Swansea City
2010/11

Swansea City
1970/71

Swansea City 2010/11

WALKING ON SUNSHINE

Keith Haynes

For Anj

Dedicated to a body of people who, in 2002, were brave
enough to stand up and be counted. People who were not
going to sit back and accept the demise of a city's
football club. These people are true fans of Swansea City
Football Club, and who had never run or coordinated
a football club before. They would never know that in
nine years they would have completed one of the greatest
journeys a football club has ever made and had themselves
become one of the most important factors in
Swansea City's history.

This is the story of how Swansea City realised their
Premier League dream.

First published 2011

The History Press
The Mill, Brimscombe Port
Stroud, Gloucestershire, GL5 2QG
www.thehistorypress.co.uk

British Library Cataloguing in Publication Data.
A catalogue record for this book is available from the British Library.

ISBN 978 0 7524 6444 2

Typesetting and origination by The History Press
Printed in Great Britain
Manufacturing managed by Jellyfish Print Solutions Ltd

Contents

Foreword
by Phil Sumbler

Swansea City is a remarkable football club. I say that not because of a trophy cabinet that is littered with silverware that you may find at Old Trafford or Anfield. Nor do I say it because we have hovered around the top two divisions for many seasons like, say, a West Brom or a Bolton Wanderers. No, I say it because ten years ago we were on the edge of oblivion. Years of mismanagement at board level had taken us to rock bottom and the club was in danger of going under.

Since that time it has been pretty much success after success. And it is fair to say that the success has gone pretty much unnoticed. Not just by the Welsh media but by the people of Swansea as well. But thanks to the starting hardcore back in 2001 we now have a story to tell which Keith will take you through in his own passionate style. It's rags to riches and one that many didn't realise was happening.

20 per cent of the club is owned by ordinary supporters through the vehicle that I head up – the Supporters' Trust. And back in 2001 this vehicle spent many hours assisting in piecing together a consortium that today forms the board of directors of Swansea City. This consortium was a group of local businessmen who – like us – were lifetime supporters of the club and who cared that it remained intact for their own families to enjoy, just as we had done in the generation before them. Friendships were formed and a club was reborn and tentatively took the first steps into its future. It was not always easy – it was never going to be – but through hard work, dedication and sometimes a slice of luck we find ourselves where we are now.

And it is not just that board of directors or the trust that share the passion for the club. Behind the scenes there is a group of people all of whom work exceptionally hard for the good of the club and share the same sense of pride at the progress that the club has made. And that is where I started; Swansea City is a remarkable football club.

I have been fortunate enough – at least I think it's fortunate – to know Keith for around fifteen years. I first met him via the early football forums on the internet when, in those very early days, he was one of the few people whose passion for the football club stood out. He was someone who was not prepared to sit back and accept decisions but questioned the management – and that kind of passion, in Keith and others, helped to shape the football club that we have today.

Over those fifteen years we have shared many a beer, many a trip, a game and many a phone conversation about the club, the performance and the transfer targets. We have worked together on books and travelled to games in the past and I genuinely see Keith as one of the 'good guys'. He is not your typical mid-forties guy – the fact he sings in a successful punk rock band gives that away – but he has a passion for the Swans that will come to the fore in this book as he tells you about the ultimate season in his own words and through his own eyes.

I wish him well with this book that for once has the fairytale ending. Please don't expect it to be a 'Once upon a time'-type account of the season that we have just witnessed. It will be passionate and hit you in extremes. However, there won't be more than a handful of people who cannot relate to at least parts of this book – because most of you will relate to it all.

Enjoy.

Phil Sumbler
Chairman, Swansea City Supporters' Trust
June 2011

Acknowledgements

Thanks to the following for making this book possible. Michelle Tilling at The History Press who has managed my passion and my words far better than most; Jon Wilsher at Swansea City FC; Phil Sumbler at the Swans Trust; my travelling companions (in no particular order) Howard of Cowbridge, Kev of Henley, Andy of Gloucester, Jamie of Belfast, Dave the weatherman from Cirencester, Ieun the twitchery chap from Droitwich, Andy Conkers from Bristol. Not forgetting The East Stand exiles and homeland Jacks who regularly put up with my rantings and outbursts most matchdays – Ian Williams (ex-Gloucester Jack) Carl Haggar (ex-Cheltenham Jack), John (who sits behind me), Mick Cannon and various Weston-super-Mare Jacks including Tom. I really couldn't leave out Jon Taylor, Darren Bradley, Simon Thomas, Jeremy Hubbard and Lucky Jimbo (all from Gloucester), and the many thousands and thousands of fans of a football club that has made the biggest journey any club and supporters could make. Finally anyone else that I have shouted with, at, or towards in the true name of Swansea City AFC.

To each and every one of you, including you reader, I thank you all.

Keith Haynes,
Summer 2011

Author's Preface

To start something new there has to be an end. In this case the end, for me, was a tense and passionate Vetch Field stadium on Saturday 3 May 2003. It was the last game of the season. Swansea City had suffered not only at the hands of many teams that season, but had also endured a six-year rite of passage to their clear and inevitable extinction. For me, the previous six years signalled everything that was wrong with football, from mismanagement of off-the-field affairs to a failure to see when someone was having you over. I am a football writer, self-proclaimed maybe, but a football writer all the same. I have been for twenty years, and before that I was the proverbial passionate Swansea North Banker . . . in fact let me be very straight with you, I have been a passionate Swansea City fan for as long as I can recall. To date a forty-year journey that became intense, went north, came back and surfaced with extreme anger when I saw the various owners of my beloved club ruining the history of something I, and many thousands of others, held dear. They would pay.

But first to that day in May 2003 – it was just one of those days. For me, it was the inevitable conclusion of a directorate at the club that had bled the city dry of its football team and its finances. Personally I don't care what anyone thinks of any owner we have had since 1997 when Doug Sharpe, too late in the day, left the club. For me they did absolutely nothing for the city's football team, and needed to be brought to book, by any method chosen by any person concerned enough to want to fight for Swansea City FC. Please place that on record. And please don't think for any moment that I was any different. I was raised on the Swansea North Bank as a kid, my fuel was football and that huge mass of popular bank was my home for many years.

I may well have had to endure a 120-mile round trip by train with many others to be a part of the Swansea story, but that is how it has always been for me. A one-way love for a city's football team, not so much the individuals who play but the fact that this old lady they called the Vetch Field and all its bit-part players actually existed. From those days of obscurity and re-election to Toshack and beyond, I grew as a child, teenager and adult. I have lost friends at football, people have died supporting Swansea City FC. That starts some serious chain reaction in certain folk, let me tell you. Did these money men (they weren't, we exposed that as well) honestly believe they would be able to walk in and blag the Swansea faithful and laugh their way to the bank? To get to their financial rewards they had to get one over on the Swansea North Bank, and few have succeeded in that onerous task. They had not done their homework, and if they thought they had, they soon learned that the school we went to was one a little more real than their plummy-voiced education suggested. I remember facing them for the first time, and thought 'you're at it, you're not genuine. I'm watching you. You fool very few here.' It didn't take long. As a kid I was dragged up and spat out through a hybrid travellers' lifestyle and poorly equipped and dangerous children's homes. I could see a wrong 'un from the off. I'm not telling you this for any other reason than you must know my mindset to understand theirs. From the age of eight I had to survive pretty much unaided – you get to know the baddies quite quickly in these situations. An adult is a person who may well help you, but then they could easily be a threat to you as well. It sharpens you up. These skills I honed over a number of years have served me well through my life, and served me well in this situation too. What annoyed me more were the supporters who were drawn in by their terminology and brief; they really didn't see the arrogant smiles behind their backs, the self-importance of these individuals' lifestyles that held no resemblance to my Swansea City ethos. These new people with messages of hope encased in a questionable canister of slow-releasing gas were doomed to fail from the start, and like all of our owners since Sharpe, they were doomed to fail. It was inevitable, they were under scrutiny from some intelligent people, people who knew of them and where they came from, and the warnings by many were heeded. And like a cold war we plotted our strategy from far-flung fields of Swansea Citydom, not just the city itself, but from all corners of the globe. We went to war. Those fans who decided they wanted to trust and believe would find themselves cast aside as time went on, when the club needed action not words, when indeed the real Swans fans stood up and had to be counted. The flag was raised and the bugle sounded, it was time to stand up and be counted. And stand up we did.

On that obscure day in May I will confess I had taken on board probably too much fuel to capably assess the footballing events as they unfolded. The reason (now I know), was purely to anaesthetise the probable outcome. It worked – I had no emotion whatsoever as I walked into the Vetch that day. Those of you that recall our beloved Vetch Field will back me up here, every time you entered the ground it was an experience. Maybe not for the coming game but what had gone before – real history bled from the walls and those piss-stained floors and terraces. The energy and the love for a team in white shirts, irrespective of the person wearing that jersey. To me it didn't matter who they were, just that they gave as much for that shirt as I would have, should I have had the opportunity. I am not a hero-worshipper of men who play football – what I am and have been for many years is a Swansea City supporter, a supporter of the team and not the individuals that have been loaned for a period of time a football strip so valuable that some would lay their lives down for it. This I suppose is where the 'wonder' of entering the ground of any team is felt. The eleven players on either side are only a part of what it is to be a supporter of Association Football. They play their part, often demoralising their own club's fans, never delivering the final masterpiece having worked so hard to canvass their ideas in many-coloured formations. Young men handed a gift, many not appreciating what they have until it is too late, but that is life itself, that is football as I know it. And why I care.

When I look back at that team, that Swansea City battalion of saints dressed in white with one objective, I see very young men, innocents abroad, never knowing that what they will do today will make real history, and add to the football gift of tomorrow. From the keeper, a certain Neil Cutler, through to the hometown boy made good James Thomas with sprinklings of Leon Britton, Alan Tate and added essence of Martinez, Johnrose and Coates. We even added a big lump of O'Leary to thicken the plot – Swansea City are ready for battle. Indeed so were Hull City – they had nothing to play for but it was clear from the start they came to send Swansea City down, because that would be the outcome, if the Swans lost this game. They would leave the Football League and their glorious history, over ninety-one years of football, would be gone. Swansea the town, the city, the club, the team, the city's guiding light would be a non-league club. A big price to pay, and a heavy one for those men in white shirts to be associated with. I doubted if that happened that we would return. I know this to be true.

The ground was full, nigh-on 10,000 supporters glaring west to the small away support that had dared to come and see their team do us no good. The atmosphere was not only extremely tense, but hate-filled as well and the looks on the faces of the stewards and police told me that anything could give today. The North Bank was packed, the ground's capacity severely reduced; well, we had our problems, but crammed as we were together this was going to be our very own version of Custer's Last Stand. It's ten minutes to three and, as is usual, the police visit the referee's dressing room. This meeting of Swansea police officers and the matchday referee and linesmen was a simple one. The referee was concerned at the delay in kick-off, and the mood of the crowd. He was told quite simply, 'The crowd are hostile, and we have to have a mind that anything could spark them off.' This was Swansea, a fearsome club with a fearsome hooligan element – let's not be coy about this – the Swansea firm as they were had a reputation to live up to and keep. And I will confess, I couldn't just sense that things were very tense, I could bloody well taste it. The referee was now not happy, something had been planted in his mind that this was a little bit more than just another game of football. If he didn't know it when he arrived, he certainly did now. If I was him I would feel I had an obligation in fair play, whatever you deem that fair play to be. But that's me. To my peers he looked scared as he walked out on to the Vetch Field turf, indeed to me he looked petrified. I'll leave it there. But make of that ten minutes before kick-off what you will.

The next 90 minutes served up the most enthralling rollercoaster of a football nightmare ride I have ever been on. Sex? You're joking – it will never come close (excuse the pun), but this was life-ending stuff. The snuff movie of Association Football unfolded before us all, and at its climax we could all be dead. At certain points during that game, as situations changed in games around the league, and most importantly at Exeter City, we were actually down and out. When Martin Reeves put Hull City 2–1 up after 25 minutes would be a good example. I'm not joking, people around me cried, and the anger increased to boiling point. By half time the rollercoaster slammed its breaks on, threw us all off track and the Swans equalised. In fact two of Swansea's goals that day came by way of the penalty spot. Thanks ref. For me one was nailed on, but the next a matter of opinion . . . with thousands of angry, screaming voices asking the question, I suppose opinions are just that. There would only be one result. Easily rationalised, but from my viewpoint I saw no rational behaviour at all. 2–2 at half time. I needed sustenance, pure alcohol to go with my pure adrenalin.

The atmosphere wasn't helped by the recent Hull City/ Swansea City rivalry where planned battles between the two sets of fans had been disrupted by local law enforcement officers on Humberside. This was after a game a few seasons before where Hull fans entered the away terrace with violence on their minds. The Swansea North

Bank needed no second invitation: they invaded the playing surface and went hell-for-leather towards the away fans.

The second half was played out on a muddy pitch, the volume cranked to eleven on the North Bank as the South Stand mobilised its adventurers who yearned for one last moment of their own making. Cue James Thomas – Swansea boy and Swansea fan. Did I tell you he was on a hat-trick? Well, he was, he had two penalties under his belt already as he headed on for Lenny Johnrose to put the Swans 3–2 up. It was bedlam, a mentalness (that probably isn't a word, I know) I've never experienced since. A thousand expressos and a hundred energy tablets exploded in everyone's brain. The ground literally shook itself free of the past six years. I've never experienced a moment like it. The concrete blocks and bricks of that old lady shone like a ray of light had been cast across them, the East Stand rose like an eagle, like a leaning tower of pride over the Vetch Field turf. Even the South Stand gave way to emotions of a football nature, and attentions diverted to the playing surface for once. It was inevitable that James Thomas would get his third goal – it was now inevitable that the three points would be Swansea City's. And it was so. On fifty-eight minutes James Thomas chipped the Hull City keeper with – what would be described, I suppose, by a Fleet Street journalist – aplomb. Other words were used that day as he swerved away to confront the North Bank and celebrate. He was a Swansea great, forever in our hearts. That man would be one of only a few deserving of some charity as a person who played for Swansea City. There are few others. Even after all I've said, he was a bit part in a bit part. But it worked for me. Swansea City had a new chapter to write.

If ever there should be a footnote to what had gone before, the end before the beginning that is, it should go here. As that day in May 2003 unfolded, a Dutch television crew filmed the events at Exeter City and Swansea City. You can find the film on the internet at times, and it's worth a look. Swansea City have had for many years a Dutch connection, and that connection stems from a friendship between one Swansea City supporter and one ADO Den

Haag supporter. Over the years, as their friendship gathered pace, so did the frequent visits of both clubs' sets of fans to each other's main event games. It has to be said, both teams do have a few less-than-genteel supporters, but don't let that take away from this story I tell you.

As this Dutch TV crew filmed the events, it was irony, or perhaps fate, that the director or co-owner, call him what you will, of Exeter City was one Michael Lewis, later to be convicted of fraud during his reign at the club. He came to Swansea City as a programme editor in about 1997, coincidentally when the first regime after Doug Sharpe took over. He and significant others never gauged the Swansea support appropriately. After he left Swansea, the fans of Exeter City were warned of his strategy. He'll give you Uri Geller and Michael Jackson my friends, as the ringmaster of your fate, he'll even say he loves the club. They took no heed, and ended up very much where Swansea City were destined. It's odd how these things pan out. Thankfully Exeter City have returned to the Football League with no thanks at all to Michael Lewis and his cohort John Russell, a man who hardly had an honest run of things at Scarborough. Both were convicted at Bristol Crown Court for fraud. At the end of the documentary they are seen to peer out of their Exeter City office window. Look closer, the window has bars on it. How very appropriate. Lewis later wrote a book about his experiences in football, I have half a mind to buy a copy, but I can't find it anywhere.

The real celebration is that after years of struggle a trust was formed by the fans of Swansea City FC. After entering a company voluntary agreement in 2002, the trust is still the focus in 2011 and 2012. The board assembled themselves in 2002 from local supporters, mainly based in Swansea, with one or two extras. The catalyst for this was a meeting in a Bristol hotel in 2002 with a number of Swansea City supporters, including myself. I headed up the main supporters' club in England, a constant thorn in previous administration's side (tell the truth Swansea owners and we will go away – it wasn't hard to grasp). Now, I know that other factors were afoot at the time, and one of the attendees that night was later to be a board member and now vice-chairman Leigh Dineen. I had much to talk with him about during those days as I did with another board member, David Morgan, a Swansea City supporter of many years. Sometimes he struggled to see my point of view, and indeed that may well be a point he would moot as well.

David Morgan cared about Swansea City, which was good enough for me at the time, although I saw many things beyond the smiles in those heady days of aggressive posturing and egotistical group-formation. We were football fans foremost – for many this was the first time they had mixed business and pleasure. Doing so can be a mental struggle when you can't think that broadly as a person, let alone as a fan. Phone calls at the time revolved around getting together a board of supporters who were worthy of recovering the club. I thought long and hard over my position, and living away from Swansea was one factor, while the fact that there was a lot of jostling for position was another. I declined the offer, and the sums of money were small. I fancied my work as a fan had been done, I had agitated enough, and could see no future for myself with regards to the higher echelons of the club. Rightly or wrongly I was happy with my life as a supporter, and whatever they achieve now they have my backing.

The board of Swansea fans had all our support and best wishes as we resurrected the club from nothing. By 'we' I mean the board and fans and the relentless work of Huw Jenkins and many others more local, including Leigh, who made sure that the club could function and hold its head high again. For that at least I thank them all.

John Van Zweden, a lifelong Swansea supporter from Holland, also contributed to his position in Swansea history and aided David Morgan to a position on the new board too. The two friends united to ensure a Swansea City future, for them and us. It's quite simple, that game against Hull City, coupled with the fans' desire to literally run out of town any person wishing to kill our club was clearly evident. These previous owners, before the fans took control of Swansea City in 2003, were never, ever going to get the new stadium they and the club desired under any stewardship other than one that could be trusted. And for one owner or another over that period, there were always elements within that stewardship at Swansea City that couldn't be trusted. Indeed, in some cases they had no integrity at all. I am proud to have harangued, demonstrated, motivated and mobilised many Swansea City supporters to the point of distraction to chase back down the M4 any pirate or misguided fool who thought us thick Swansea City fans were a push-over. Their words, not mine. Like night became *day*, we were utterly relentless.

I spent hours and hours with many others annihilating every overture and freebie that was offered by previous owners at the club, and exposing them at every turn. Many said 'Oh be careful Keith, they have major legal back-up.' Really? As Michael Moore has stated many times 'Judge me as a person, and ask yourself this. If I am not telling the truth, why am I not in the courts of this land answering as to why?' What more can I say? And when it was done, when they were all despatched to their miserable lives elsewhere, I and many others were happy. Strong words? I don't care, they messed with my club and as a highly motivated group led by highly motivated Swansea City supporters from every location, our tentacles spread wide. Trust me, the support we had from on high was unbelievable. If I told you that revered business people, judges, police and councillors backed our battle plan to rid the club of this continuous cancer, would you be surprised? Don't be – they did – and more and more joined the support network, promising unbelievable back-up if required. The powers-that-be supported the troops on the ground, an army of hope that had battalions and battalions of support across the football divide. Yes, we even had spirited messages from the FAW, from individuals who also spied wrongdoers but couldn't do much more than offer their support. Or should I say were fearful of doing so, not that we were in any way in fear – of anyone. To all those souls, known and otherwise, you know who you are, and this makes Swansea City v Hull City in 2003 even more special, because we stood up, and *you* were counted. Without fear and without reward. Others since 2003 may have gained a reward for their efforts – I don't blame them, but I will leave those people who laid a claim to my club prior to the revolution with this sentiment. Take it how you will, with sugar or sweetener, I don't care. I mean these words so much.

To those owners and people of the darker days of SCFC: if you were so credible, if you were so believable, why do you think you didn't get the new stadium and all the rewards that are evident at Swansea City today? Think long and hard, and best keep quiet methinks, there was and is plenty more I could have said. I collect evidence well, and know the real remit for a proper investigation. Fear not. But surely the question burns? Why did they not achieve what the supporters' board has achieved? Well, the answer is in this sentence – supporters – that's first. And it shouldn't be lost on anyone. The very minute, if not almost immediately, the trust and fans' board was formed then the building of the Liberty Stadium began. Coincidence? Or just what happens when there are too many questions left unanswered and too many arrogant statements made that eventually when exposed clearly display an agenda even the daftest of fans could see. Johnny Hollins' Barmy Army? Don't make me laugh.

The Liberty Stadium got fully underway as soon as the board members of Swansea City could be trusted – people who had the club and not their wallets at heart. And that's the real answer, so suffer all ye who went before, for it is I and those who care who really won the war, and every time I think of you, I laugh. I laugh very loudly indeed. For a beginning there has to be an end. And the end was Hull City in May 2003, we shed our skins and rid ourselves of those who tried to harm the city's club. We built a new future, the fans and the board, which even today can be proud of the work that has been done – and indeed continues today.

Chapter One

Walking on Anger

I t's May 2010, and to be honest the prospect of even thinking about football doesn't actually fill me with any type of positivity. It was only a few weeks earlier that the team I support, Swansea City, once again fell by the wayside at the last minute when a play-off place was almost confirmed. To be completely truthful at this point I was getting really annoyed with one or two things that were happening at the club as the season progressed. The manager, Paulo Sousa, had annoyed me; the press citing any number of players' dislikes and differences with the club had annoyed me; the lack of anything coming from the club regards any of this had annoyed me, and overall when I think about it now – I was bloody annoyed. Anger management should have been a route out. But should I really have been angry? I shouldn't have been, I know. When we were first promoted to the Championship only two seasons previously, I would have been happy to have stayed there forever. So what had changed?

The first thing that changed was the departure of Roberto Martinez after our first Championship season ended in 2009: now that annoyed me. I ran up a £120 telephone bill while on holiday in Sri Lanka as it all unfolded. Then the appointment of Paulo Sousa annoyed me, purely from a football point of view because I didn't feel he would contribute anything other than negativity to our side. I may have been proved wrong as our second season in the Championship moved forwards, but I knew he wouldn't hold water, and indeed over the last fifteen games or so of the season I doubt if we won three games. I'm annoyed about that more than anything. My view at the time was that you don't loan players to your rivals. Now Blackpool, when Stephen Dobbie was loaned at the end of January

2010, may well not have been considered a rival, indeed Dobbie may not have been considered a first-team player. However, as a result of some magnificent loan signings and an astute manager in Ian Holloway they soon became our closest rivals. And the Dobster was instrumental in this. More annoyance.

Holloway is quoted as walking away from Swansea City's stadium the season before and admitting that the way Swansea played their game was the only way to get out of the Championship. He quickly put the blueprint into play and before you knew it Blackpool were beating the country's finest in the Premier League. Fair play Ian. 'Cheers for the striker who scored decisive goals against Plymouth and Doncaster and got us to Wembley when all looked lost,' says our friend in his distinctive West Country accent.

A mate of mine has recently stated that Dobbie's loan to Blackpool didn't affect the season. I will repeat his stats: he scored 5 goals in 10 games (Blackpool won two of those games he scored in the season proper), and he scored against Forest in the play-offs to take Blackpool to Wembley. Not affecting the season? Really? There's another reason I'm annoyed, and I think the Swansea chairman – from what I am hearing – isn't too happy either. And I don't blame him. Things may be announced soon.

Swansea City's board has built itself up on what has gone on before – there is no way they want to be the reason why the club falls into administration again. There are three reasons for this: they are Swansea City fans, they have egos that would be forever dented and finally they would never be able to buy a drink in Morgans Hotel again. So, with Huw Jenkins guiding things as such, and admirable back-up in the board room, the last thing I will do is point the finger there. I know that they have my club at heart, and support them solidly in doing what they believe to be right for our team. I mean, here we are in the Championship, hardly failures are they? I've had my eye on them, mind you. Recent history tells us that the regime at the club will give the current manager, whoever that may be, a decent shot at things. They will get upset from time to time, we all do, but they have given all the managers of recent years a fair shout. And they have been good quality managers at that. But Paulo didn't fill me with any sort of confidence – he was a great player, but then so was Bobby Charlton.

At that time I'd heard that Paulo hadn't been in touch with the club since the end of the season, and things weren't as tickety-boo as all would have you believe. This led me to think 'sack him, I don't care'. He blew it when it was on a plate. Heartless, I know, but I was so angry I really couldn't give a flying scone for Paulo Sousa . . . and Bruno thingy, his assistant. You will find, from time to time as you read this book, that my mood is up and down quite a lot. My pure view is one of a fan who loves laughing at the wide world as we career along poking fun at other teams, especially those cases down the road. The story is often interspersed with moments of pure elation, downright anger, followed by further periods of remorse and total unhappiness. Yes, it's called being a football fan. And quite similar to marriage I'll have you know. Bear with me though, this is a Swansea journey.

In a more reflective mood I can see why Paulo wouldn't be going just yet, when you look at the season and the little we spend as a club on players, the whole adventure of the 2009/2010 season seems a success. Maybe someone will come in and poach him from us? We may even get a few quid compo! The news is telling me that Hull City want a certain Nigel Pearson as their new manager, thus leaving Leicester City in the hunt for a new guiding light. I hope he is Portuguese. I have been a bit of a pain at times over the years in relation to certain football matters, especially when my club was being pillaged by all sorts of dodgy types. I made a few remarkable acquaintances along the way, though – indeed I met some really interesting people. Over the years as I wrote books, and certain other newspapers wanted a few more column inches, things got quite positive. I suppose the real problem for me was the success of Swansea City. Put simply, as soon as we drove the thieves away from the club, leading up to the fans taking over, I went away too. The dodgy elite not being there stopped my moaning and constant haranguing of club owners who would do us down. My talents were no longer needed. I was removed from the club programme as was Phil Sumbler; that was a relief, I didn't have an agenda any more and didn't need to keep punching from the inside. I was disappointed that no thanks were ever conveyed, but maybe these new owners, these fans from the terraces, were as wary of me and my untempered rationale as those we had just ousted?

I have kept many acquaintances in football; they have proven a lifeline when I have become bored in recent times. As I complete my FA agents' licence (just for the hell of it) this has proved very beneficial. I mean the removal of Paulo Sousa was a little clearer to me having spoken to the very agents who had dealt with Swansea City of late. The fees we paid via Paulo that season were quite high. For me, now, this indicates a club desperate to bring in players when the manager was either failing to do so or not able to do so owing to his lack of knowledge. It has to be so.

I got a message from a well-known Welsh London-based journo . . . 'Writing a book is it? They won't like it at Swansea boy – they were never sure about you down there, even though your lot were instrumental in getting them on the board.' Well, I know differently. We aided their move from the terraces to the boardroom, but so did so many others – they took the poisoned chalice, and since then have worked wonders. I personally don't care who likes me and who doesn't, no matter if they be board members or Swansea fans. I couldn't give a toss. That has never been my goal in life – to be liked. I have my friends and I have my family, which is all that matters.

So I am sold; I am on the road to glory once again with Swansea City FC – the book is a goer, and there is a number of interested publishers. Remember I'm only writing a book, it won't stop the world turning! The topic will bore some (or maybe most) but they haven't heard from the real me, ever. I have always been too edited and too cornered to give a real fan's view. This will be different though. It won't upset anyone, don't get me wrong, but fans are fans and they know how it goes out there in midweek in the snow, and in pre-season gubbins at, let me see, oh, Hereford. That's the first one for me, then, Edgar Street in the summer. I suppose it could be worse. But not much.

The thread about Paulo Sousa leaving the club is gathering momentum, and if he does I'll have to put up with all the rumour and speculation about who gets the job next. Maybe we should have given the job to Gus Poyet – he was my first choice to be fair – and now cementing things at Brighton. And that's not a bad shout – who do we go for? Who would want this Swansea chalice? My view is that not many managers would, after all we would be on our third manager in as many seasons. It's difficult. Then all hell breaks loose, Paulo is a wanted man. First it's West Ham, then it's Leicester. An astute chairman would sit on his hands, methinks. One minute we are looking at sacking him, the next we are back on the gravy train. Guillem Bauza has been released as well, so the squad is being trimmed in the manager's absence. And players are being lined up as well, and judging by the names I have been given, Paulo doesn't even know where these teams play, let alone who their players are.

15 May 2010

And then Besian Idrizaj died. I was shocked. I saw it on Ceefax. 'Swansea City striker is dead'. I pressed in the page numbers . . . who is it? Trundle?, Gorka? even Kuqi? When I read his name, it didn't register; Idrizaj had played only one full game for the Swans – he was one in the making for us – he had made two substitute appearances as well. He only scored one recorded full-time goal for Luton Town while on loan in 2007 from Liverpool. We got him on a free from Liverpool and I had seen him twice in a Swans shirt. He had a lovely touch and seemed to be fitting in with the Swansea City way. Besian was definitely one for the future. The tributes poured in, and another bright star was remembered. Alan Curtis said it all – he is the right man to say the best things when the club needs to, especially at times like this. He stated that Besian was going to make a real impact on the coming season, and from the brief glimpse I had, I really had to agree. But I couldn't say it like Curt. My thoughts were more simple, less – thoughtful. Besian Idrizaj died in his sleep, there was no rolling drum or conspiracy theory. He did have some medical issues at Liverpool but they were analysed and all was good for a bright future. For all of us Swansea supporters it was a shock. He died at home, with his family. If there was to be a place to be where any of us died, I would say at home with our family would be the answer.

Football anger and football misery are put into context again. And life itself becomes far more hopeful, if not a tad more fragile as a result.

May and June is a mad time at football clubs and because so little happens the rumours are rife. Supporters want whole squads assembled by the middle of June! Madness! Summer 2010 is no different – in fact it feels worse than usual. The fans have no scores to settle and argue about after a weekend of football, and as a result the rumour mill starts to crank itself into life. So far the club is losing Dobbie to Blackpool, Sousa is now linked to Hull City, Ashley Williams is linked with just about every Premier League club and Darren Pratley is about to sign for Nottingham Forest for the fifth time this year. I'll add a few more for you – Neil Danns is signing from Crystal Palace, Jordi Gomez and Jason Scotland are coming back, and when Sousa leaves Paul Tisdale will be the new Swans manager. They obviously don't know Tisdale, because I know he wouldn't want to be our manager. I have my spies, in fact I don't need them – I know for a fact he will not leave Exeter City. I mean it's not even time for the play-off final and all this is being talked about in every Swansea drinking house. What I do know is that a terrific player by the name of Neil Taylor at Wrexham would love to sign for us, and that Leon Britton is going to be moving on. A signing-on fee, and a big increase in cash each week is the incentive for any player but Leon is going because he can't work with Paulo; that is my belief. Taylor is coming in because he doesn't care who he plays for in the Championship – after all, a job in the Championship is a far better job than one in the Conference at Wrexham. If he signs he could well pick up four grand a week, a little more than he gets at Wrexham I would have thought. That, my friends, is not rocket science. What is, though, is the ever-evolving, press-driven, Cardiff-based arrogance of the determination to upset the apple cart further at Swansea City. I read a list of players that if borrowed or purchased will bankrupt the club this season at the new Cardiff City stadium. Part of me thinks 'good riddance', but I know the true and genuine Cardiff fan would have a huge gap appear in their lives if this was to happen . . . and anyway, they are worth a good few points each season, so why take that away from Swansea City?

I also think that some football fans need a little educating at times, myself included, as to the ways of the movement of players between clubs. But I am learning, quicker than most. Get ready Huw, I may well be sitting in front of you in the coming years talking through the next big Swansea City signing! There is no other industry that is as clever at working around the signing-on guidelines of players than football. When loan windows appear we see players signing 'potential' deals over three years, when really the loan window is there for just that – for players to be loaned. But the term 'loaned with a view to a three-year deal' has cropped up regularly in recent times. So clubs are not stupid, and Swansea City are not stupid either. Unless a player needs to be snapped up immediately, a club is hardly likely to sign them in May when they know they can do so in July thus saving two months' wages, are they? Swansea know this and most astute clubs do, too. At Swansea we do have other factors influencing players outside of agents and media speculation, and that is pay scales. Blackpool are very similar in this respect. Swansea City players like Leon Britton will not be on vast sums of money to ply their trade; in Leon's case he was happy enough to play at League Two level when he joined us on a free transfer from West Ham.

He, like many before him, found a home for himself in South Wales, and a bond with the area. He wanted to sign. As a result he built a relationship with the supporters and found himself able to supply a decent wage for his family. Everyone's happy. My thoughts are that he should be happy now, but when money is not so much of a factor, and you are not getting games, then common sense says that Leon will move on regardless.

As Swansea City progressed, his wages kept pace with the club's success, reaching the point whereby he could be about to go out of contract and demand far more money for the level he was at. That is simple economics, but those simple economics will not match Swansea City's desire to pay him an amount of money, be that £8,000 a week as an example, for a two- or three-year contract. Most of us would be happy to be on £32,000 a month – I think all of us would just about manage on that. However, if another club is waving a cheque for £14,000 a week, what is the player expected to do? All of a sudden they are on a three-year deal worth in excess of £1,500,000. Then there is the big signing-on fee. This could be £150,000 at least for an out-of-contract player (and agent). Economics at this level mean the player will probably leave.

In this case Sheffield United are keen to sign Leon; he is available on a free, which means a very decent signing-on wedge for him as well. Leon and agent are happy, Sheffield United are happy, they have got one of the best midfielders in the league, and to be honest Swansea fans should be happy as well. He has got us to a position where we are in good health on the pitch, and has taken the opportunity to make himself secure for the rest of his life as a result. But it didn't work like that for everyone. My view is that Leon will be very unhappy at Sheffield United, the ball constantly in the air will do his neck in for a start. At this the Swansea City fans are very annoyed, almost furious in some circumstances, but nothing like the feeling experienced at the departure of Roberto Martinez. Leon had done his bit, and the 50/50 split in emotion meant the more reflective supporter could wish him well. I just feel today, as his signing is announced, that he has made a very bad choice professionally based on a bigger pay packet. Granted Sheffield United are a bigger club than Swansea City, if attendances and history are reviewed, but are they really now, today, as we speak of him leaving? Is size important compared to achievement in the future? I think Leon will live very quickly to regret this move – maybe his agent won't, but Leon will.

Leon Britton going to Yorkshire is one thing, but with every real story comes other madder and badder ones. Sousa is now linked with Panathinaikos, and Swansea with an Orient player who probably doesn't even know where Swansea is. Stephen Quinn, the Sheffield United player, won't be coming to the Liberty either, despite the media's best efforts to convince us all. And mid-June approaches us with news that Darren Pratley will be a Celtic player by the weekend. I suppose at moments like these it is time for a chairman to make a few comments, even make an announcement. In Swansea's case, Huw Jenkins is the man for the job – he is probably the only person at the club on 16 June, with the sun beating down on the bay and holiday time now approaching at full throttle. He states that there will be no big-money signings this season. Now what do you class as 'big money'? In Swansea terms that could be a £300,000 buy from League Two, or indeed £500,000 for Craig Beattie. It's difficult to work out what he means exactly, purely because the Welsh press have broken the story. Make of that what you will but there is an element of journalism in Wales that is firmly entrenched in the Cardiff City camp, so any chance of a news story that deflates near-neighbours Swansea City will be most welcome. For me I see this as the opportunity they need.

Huw has had more practice at talking to the media over the past seven years or so. At first he wasn't very good at it, he may well admit this himself – he said things that didn't help when matters were considered serious. On this occasion he puts his story forward well, and consolidates the thoughts of the reader with clear comments, and I know that these comments have not been misquoted either. The thrust of this chairman's message is a simple one – once again we as a club will not be placed in any serious debt just to progress. Cardiff City down the road is a good example, as I write, of a club who lurch from financial crisis to financial crisis to appease their support, and the local media who constantly analyse them. This proves my point that this board do not want to be responsible for the demise of the club, and will not be placed in question by the supporters if extreme debt became an issue. Better to be criticised for running a tight and proper ship than be the reason for the club going down the pan again. Simple logic.

So no big money signings at Swansea this summer, and to be honest I don't want them and their entourage anywhere near my club. The skills of Carlos Tevez are welcome everywhere, but not his desire to earn more money than the national debt of Argentina. For me, I am happy that Huw is sitting there pondering the club's future when most of us are thinking about two weeks away in the sun.

On the point of players leaving, the grass has been greener for many over the years – it is a case though of 'where are they now' and maybe 'what did they achieve?' Fede Bessone has decided that Leeds United is the place for him and he leaves on a free transfer, that's two players off the main menu in a week. More of an anti-pasti to be honest, nothing players contributing even less to the Swansea cause. Huw will be happy, it gives us more possibility for movement as the month progresses. Bessone won't succeed at Leeds, he wasn't that great last season, and has found his feet this time around. I get the feeling he will fall flat on his face like so many before him have as well . . . other Leeds players who were once flying Swans.

Talking of players who have endeared themselves to Swansea's support, Lee Trundle wants to sign a deal but my contacts tell me that a certain Welsh league club are very keen to sign him. At this point I started to laugh at the absurdity of Lee Trundle playing to crowds of 300 on a Saturday afternoon. Then I thought, it's that absurd, it may be true. I made a phone call, and ye gods, it is true! Trundle is about to be offered a fortune to play for Neath. I'm astounded. I tell my good friend Howard of Cowbridge the news, and he asks if I have been drinking in the afternoon again. I said I had, but that had nothing to do with the truth. I try all sorts of conspiracy theories to work out what has happened here and end up with the obvious. The thing here is that the current owner has a lot of money and likes football. Yeah right, I hear you say, and I say it too. No matter how much you fire it round your head it's the same answer. Lee Trundle is an eagle. And for those who don't know what I'm on about – I mean he is a Neath player with European qualification on his mind. I am not stupid, and before the news settles as fact I am straight down the bookies to get some hard-earned on Neath making Europe. Top three will do it, and I get twenty notes on the bookies' table. This is not as absurd a bet I made last season that Swansea City would qualify for the Champions League before the end of the 2013/14 season, though. We can all dream for twenty quid.

Among the things that annoy me a lot in football are players who don't see clearly what they have been given, and what they could achieve. It goes back, perhaps, to all those players who have left the club never to be heard of again. Stupidity is blind, but then some would have you believe that certain footballers are not the brightest. I disagree with this, having been privy to the lives of a number of players; they are, in the main, astute and somewhat worldly wise, but of course there are exceptions. In the case of Andrea Orlandi I see a player who came to us with a pedigree of not achieving a great deal, irrespective of the clubs he had played for, including Barcelona. He was offered a lifeline in the English game by Roberto Martinez which he took, and he took a reasonable salary too. In return, well, in return I am yet to be convinced. So when I read about him stalling on contracts and getting the chairman involved in media speculation on timeframes I get a bit annoyed. Now Orlandi is not a stupid man, I can see that by the way he dresses. And I can also see a player who wants what is best for himself and his future. But of course when I see my club as the focus for this bettering of oneself I do get a bit angry – again. Especially when that player has done little to display what he is about other than play the waiting game. If I had my way today, Andrea Orlandi would be down the road. The Swansea boot extending to the far reaches of his well-manicured backside, I feel offended his agent and he would treat us so badly after the push forward Swansea City have given him.

The last week of this perilously hot and bothering month of June takes us all to Leicester City yet again, and Milan Mandaric spouting the tune. This is a man I have watched over the years and he reminds me of a wound-up clockwork toy. That's not meant to be insulting, I don't want a contract taken out on my garden gnomes you understand, but he does annoy a lot of football fans. Except those at Leicester, no doubt. But as a club, Leicester City – I have to say I don't like them. I'll explain this again later. It's not a racial thing of course – it's purely football hatred, nothing more. Moving on – Mandaric has uttered those loving words, 'We have not ruled out a move to bring Paulo Sousa to Leicester.' Well Milan, me old mucker, my car is warmed up, I have a few hours to kill, would you like me to drop him off at Forest East services? I reckon Huw may pay the petrol.

The good news amid all this posturing and puffing out of chests is that a real footballer, who sees very clearly his destiny and future, has signed for the Swans; Wrexham's Neil Taylor is a Jack at last. He has everything we need in his locker, and for me will be a very good signing for us as next season progresses. I'm told we paid £42,000 for him, maybe £150,000, but in any event he is a great player, with great potential. I just hope this all doesn't go to his head as the season and his contract progresses. Huw's statement that we wouldn't be spending big is coming true, but who needs to when quality like Neil Taylor is sitting in the shop window for all to ignore?

Premier League managers like Ferguson and Wenger seem to miss sourcing the real lower-league gems, preferring DVDs and agents' fees. It makes me smile, and for football's sake I am sure for some it makes them cry too. It's good for Swansea City, but it's an appalling fact that many players have missed out on very decent careers based on the way the game is run today – football is just too lazy to see and to know what's happening in front of their noses. And when the media and fans complain, they don't like it. But they continue to feed the very people the money they need to be lazy. It's mad. It is all about money, though, and even though the World Cup is underway, with little interest from me at all, I spy the FIFA delegates and crew, and feel a chill of cold at the sight of their overindulged, bloated fat-cat frames. Just how well-paid are their bloated bellies, and where indeed does this FIFA thing begin and end? Financially. The world game is in disarray; that is why I love Swansea, and I love the way it is run. There are elements of honesty at my club that Sepp Blatter wouldn't recognise if it was given to him in a brown paper bag. I thought it wonderful when an acquaintance down Swansea way said to me 'I think he is a mental bud, no class see, just greed.' Summed up perfectly.

One final point on Neil Taylor . . . did the conversation go like this when Paulo, fresh from weeks away from the club, had his first meeting with the board?

'Mr Chairman, I have been working very hard these past few weeks, and I think we should sign Neil Taylor from Wrexham. He has all the qualities we need for the future. Oh, and Scott Donnelly at Aldershot is another key signing for us.'

It just didn't happen. But they signed for Swansea City, in his absence from the club, and just as talk gathered momentum of him leaving. For me Paulo is a coach at best, a manager in the Martinez mould he is not, and I am hearing, contrary to what the club are saying, that he knows full well where Forest East services are, and indeed what junction he needs to turn off on the M1 to get to the Walkers Stadium.

Chapter Two

My Mate Phil:
Manager of Swansea?

Before July has a chance to sniff the backside of June, Paulo Sousa, after much torment, has gone, and it seems that it hasn't cost the club a penny. In fact we may have got that compo too. I don't mind how much, I knew that any money gained here would be well paid out to make the chairman full-time, and to compensate him for the work he and the board have done to keep our club on an even keel. I suppose my only reckless thought here would be, why don't they (the board) announce who is getting what and when, then all the fans would know, and all the fans would with good grace say 'fair play, you deserve it.' The last thing the board would want is supporters believing they were doing their work for little or no reward, and then finding out that wasn't true. It's an integrity issue for me, but then I do think deeply about these things. Others either don't or couldn't care.

The managerial hot seat at Swansea could be in for a bit of a hard time if this whole issue of appointing a new manager isn't handled properly. The board should know by now they are being analysed a little bit more than usual by certain quarters, and I won't include myself in this. I don't think they see me or my project as a threat, in fact I know that they don't. What they do see as a threat is another uprising as in 2002, and yes, if that was to happen, they would then see me as a threat. And I would be as well. But there is no need for this conjecture on the future, as we have a shortlist of managers, and I am sure if those managers are approached professionally they will be chomping at the bit to take the job. The usual Welsh press nonsense ensues.

Paul Tisdale, Chris Coleman, Gareth Southgate, Gary Speed, Sean O'Driscoll, Graeme Jones, John Hartson, Jim Magilton, Dean Holdsworth, Bobby Davison, Gianfranco Zola, Nigel Adkins, Brendan Rodgers, Billy Reid and my mate Phil Sumbler were all connected to the manager's job at Swansea. The latter even got support from some of the lesser-spotted brain dead on his Swansea City forum. If anyone needs any further proof that manipulating the media is as easy as feeding kids sweets, then this is it. I'll leave it there, but Phil actually got into the reckoning, and he found it as funny as I did. I could break down all the potential managers here, but I won't, they in the main are no-hopers when it comes to the job at Swansea. Tisdale was never coming, we knew that already. Coleman was recently sacked by a poor Coventry and to end up like them at this point would be a terrible thing for the club. O'Driscoll probably wanted to come to Swansea but compensation would have proved the stumbling block, so it's back to the Swansea City model again.

Who is available, are they at a club? How do we get them for nothing? For me, and the bookies won't thank me for this, there is only one candidate – Brendan Rodgers. A young and reasonably successful football person, with good contacts who is pretty keen to prove Watford and Reading wrong, and be a success at Swansea. It's a no-brainer, and the bookies took a hiding for their ignorance and stupidity in not seeing clearly what was in front of their eyes. While they were sucked into the idea of Gareth Southgate (there was no way he would take the job, he is too busy spitting crisps everywhere on TV), Brendan was being silently touted by the board and Huw Jenkins. The fans got all uppity about the length of time that was being taken to appoint a new manager (forgive me but it was only two weeks!) And the media fuelled their anger by talking complete and utter bullshit. It was magnificent to read, and even more magnificent to see the media turn on Rodgers almost immediately he was appointed. I could see a man desperate to prove everyone wrong, he had that steely glint in his eye, he was hungry and wanted success. In Swansea

City he had a vehicle to prove this to all, and in Huw Jenkins he had an ally to work with. Huw, I am sure, saw a man who was flexible enough to see what the club wanted, and would go further than the other potential candidates to work with the club. Brendan spoke well, he looked a tad scared at his first few press conferences, a little like a rabbit caught in the headlights, but that would change I was sure. He had desire, and not a street car was in sight.

The club's financial position was made clear to Brendan, and the expectations on him to work within that framework, so he was under no illusions. The board had learned well from the past. He was fully briefed on the club, and what the full picture was at that time. He was fully versed in the history and recent salvation of the city's football team and I could see a relationship forming immediately – everyone seemed more at ease, and the angry phone calls from anonymous sources stopped. All of a sudden Swansea City was a happy story again. No news in that is there?

As soon as the manager merry-go-round was sorted out, the player merry-go-round stories began again – funny that. Angel Rangel is off to Blackpool (part one) and Pratley is off to Forest (he didn't say much to stop the speculation – hence the speculation). I do know how these stories start – indeed maybe I know one or two who start them. We have already spoken about press manipulation, but players can go some way at times to put these rumours to bed. He chose not to. Tamas Priskin is linked with the club again, and then I see a price tag of £400,000 and think about the chairman's clear message back in June. He won't be coming, that's for sure. If Swansea City are to pay money out along those lines it will be for a player of far more quality. I get a phone call from a friend up Newcastle way, and I'm intrigued. Scott Sinclair wants to learn Welsh.

Football is back as well, albeit on friendly terms. An easy victory over Cheltenham is gently gained with little effort, and this signals to me some confidence in the team which is confirmed by Garry Monk's statement that Rodgers is doing perfectly well on the training pitch and the players love him. Excellent, and cheers for that Garry. Mark Yates, the Cheltenham manager, is so much in awe of the Swansea style of play he is seen leaving the ticket office after the game with a season ticket.

Jack Cork and Brian Stock are linked to us, but I get the feeling that Brendan has one big target for the start of the season, and with all due respect to these guys, it won't be either of them. By comparison none are good enough. Swansea City need some real injection of enthusiasm, and the man for the job is Scott Sinclair. Huw knows as well that the priority for the season is survival, the Championship is a nice place to be, but some of us do dream of other lands and other places to travel to. And by that I mean upwards not downwards.

I am so happy with Rodgers' appointment that when I see Gary Speed at Sheffield United I become even happier. Never could there be two more different people touted for the same job – how incredible is that? They're so different, and so far apart in their footballing mindsets. I can't see how Speed and Rodgers were even compared; the apprenticeship of Rodgers at Chelsea and his study of the game in Spain, places him in top spot every time. It was a toss-up between Brendan and Billy Reid for the job in the end. Reid declined, and said he wanted to stay at Hamilton. For once words fail me, what is wrong with people? But his negative response is in my opinion a gold nugget. We have the manager we need to survive, as Huw so concisely puts it. The press report that Alan Tate is now going to Sheffield United, I speak with a member of said 'press' and ask where he gets his information from, and he states he cannot divulge his sources. Trust me, he hasn't got any – Alan is going nowhere. But what a miserable trick to play on the new manager just to unsettle him so early on. The Welsh press can be as devious as they are easy to read at times. And all in the name of Cardiff of course. That is how I feel, as I said you will get this as I see it, uncovered, and untainted. If I put too much thought into it I probably wouldn't be so responsive.

Craig Beattie, bless him, is stating today, as we hurtle towards the new season, that goals will be his game this time around. I do feel for him, he has had more injuries than Glen Hoddle and Darren Anderton put together. This is his time, if ever there is to be a time for Craig. I wish him well and hope he can perform. It is consistency that has let him down – consistency that is, in playing five games in a row with a goals return attached. Last season he scored three goals and had an injury-littered time, if he doubles that this time around he should see that as a result. However, it is his fitness that is key. But it's goals we need at Swansea from such an expensive signing, not promises where one has failed before. I hope he hasn't duped our Brendan too much! Fast on the heels of Craig is another Swan looking to impress, this time it is Cedric van der Gun and he is stating he is up for it as well. Agents are busy briefing their players on what to say and when, so well-timed comments are in abundance as the merciless press lap it all up. Now Angel Rangel is off to Blackpool yet again: it's relentless, but Cardiff City only have to appear on the Championship stage this season because they are signing more loan players at such exorbitant costs than even I, as their biggest admirer, could imagine. The league is theirs to take and win by all accounts. Dave Jones can hold court as much as he likes, but if this lot don't do it, he is most certainly down the road. Craig Bellamy indeed.

Andrea Orlandi has signed a contract today for two years. I don't think he will be a main feature if we are to be injury-free and at full strength, but we do have the League and FA Cups to participate in. Now I am about to go pop. I get very protective of my club when I see players like Andrea and Darren Pratley, and even Angel Rangel, taking advantage of their positions. I see these people as good footballers, but not indispensible players. Maybe key to an extent to our immediate future, but in no way should we be used or abused in this way by them or their agents. I am angry when this happens, and get very emotional, thinking 'If you don't like it – go: I don't want you sweating anywhere near a pure white Swansea jersey.' This is why I am not connected to my beloved club in any capacity other than as a fan. I reckon the amount of players I would have been rolling about the floor with by now would be in the fifties. Fair play to managers, maybe it's their wage packet that stops them doing that. In the case of Brian Laws, I don't like him or rate him as a manager at all, but he has had his moments – especially at Scunthorpe. His desire to get the last word in usually ended up in a fight. That is why I am not able to mix business with my passion. I rely on a clear and cool head most days, but when it is tinged with Swansea City my decision-making can be flawed.

It is the last week of July and I am gearing up for a late summer start to the football campaign. England were rubbish in the World Cup (again) and Englanders one and all are dazed and confused. The part-time football fans who follow the big glory games can now pack away their face paints and silly hats and look towards other golden moments, like Wimbledon for instance. The comments of Rooney towards the world's cameras after yet another disappointing defeat sum him up along with the 'England must win at all costs' mentality. How can they? They aren't good enough. When will people realise this?

I need a release for my anger, it's boiling inside and tearing me apart. Then Angel declares his love for Swansea, and I see right through it. I need a football fix, I need to hold players like this dear again, close to my heart. I don't want my numerous and many contacts plying me with information that will lead me all over the place this week and next. I am busying myself trying to get some info on Sinclair and a possible move to Swansea City. The non-believer in me thinks that we only got Brendan in to get players like him, and a few others. I am hearing names like Daniel Sturridge and various attempts on an Italian name. This makes me look closer to see Fabio Borini in the mix with Scott Sinclair. Both would be available to us for a million. The acquisition of Scott is a no-brainer, and Borini a big risk. I can't see us going for both, but Sinclair would be a cracking signing. And Sturridge would be too, get these two in and let me tell you Cardiff City's signings will appear insignificant. Going a step further I truly believe that Sinclair is as good as Bellamy. He just needs an arm round him and some love, unlike Wayne Rooney. A player who can perform without the Sousa factor is the man who took Blackpool into the play-offs, one Stephen Dobbie. He is Rangers mad, but don't hold that against him (certain elements of our support most certainly won't). And for me, if his head is right he will become a season's best player along with Nathan Dyer. I am trying to convince myself to some extent, but I see the desire in Dobbie's eyes that I see in Rodgers' as well. That glint of warrior passion that Swansea City thrives upon and seeks in every person connected to the cause. We want winners, not sinners, team players, not one-man-bands spouting their own agenda. Dobbie is the man for the job for me.

The squad run around Holland as usual. Obviously Paulo wasn't interested in using his international contacts to format a good pre-season tour, further proof if any was needed that talk is cheap and he had no interest in staying at Swansea after the end of the previous season. A further return to Palamos where Roberto Martinez earned his coin in 1993 just may kill a few of us off once and for all. The tour of 2009 will live long in the memory for many of us, and for me and the 1,500 or so who made the journey to northern Spain last year, the prospect of another week like that doesn't bear thinking about. It was fantastic, though. I can't say anymore than that. Cloudy, fantastic like.

I am pleased that this year we hastily put together a pre-season tour in Holland, it means that, as I have experienced this before, I don't have to go, and will save some football points with my decidedly jaded other half for the season to come. Neil Taylor forgot his passport en route and eventually mentioned it on the bus on the way to the airport. Now I know he isn't used to international-type things, but you're looking to impress your new manager mate, come on. I am hearing that Kemy Agustien is available for the tour and will feature at some point as a trialist, he has been whispered about before, but now the club's coaching staff gets to see him properly. He isn't a bad player and even featured for Birmingham City a few seasons back. Maybe he has that steely grit we need in midfield? He is like a Mercedes when he runs, gliding over the turf and destructive in the tackle – I like his style of play as much as I admire his ability.

An easy 4–1 win against VV Haaglandia eased the players into the bonding and winning process on Dutch soil and we all hoped it would extend into the season. This was quickly followed by a 9–1 demolition of VCS, whom I have never heard of, and bless them all for turning up and adding to the tour party as hundreds of Jacks booted footballs about the astroturf at half time. They were joined by several hundred ADO Den Haag supporters as well. You need to read on to find out about this band of brothers from the Hague.

Now at this point it may be time for a bit of a history lesson. I have mentioned the link between Swansea City and ADO Den Haag which started when John Van Zweden wrote to the club back in 1982 for a pen pal. He got two responses and came over to forge that friendship and has been a 100 per cent Jack ever since. A remarkable story? His desire to see the Swans play increased as he got older and he combined his football life with ADO Den Haag, his local and more high-profile club, some would say. The yellow and green of Alles Door Oefening Den Haag is seen at most Swans games, and for the bigger fixtures literally hundreds of Dutch football fans make the pilgrimage to the Liberty to see the Swans play. The first time I saw any link would have been at the Swansea v Liverpool FA Cup fixture in 1990, when there was a huge yellow and green flag draped over the east stand at Swansea, and then later in Cardiff for the Welsh Cup final against Wrexham. Swansea City supporters often make the trip over to the Netherlands as well to watch ADO play. This is the incredible thing about football, people like John, who has more than a fan's interest in Swansea City (he bursts with pride when he speaks of the club) is now on the board at the Liberty and runs a Swansea City/ADO Den Haag museum jam-packed full of cherished football memories extending back many, many years in the Hague. This is an incredible building, and if you are in Holland, you must contact Jon and check it out.

I suppose I should finish off the pre-season jaunt with the game against ADO. Swansea lost 1–0 in a gentle game in considerably difficult conditions. No team seemed to want to take a grip of the game, the friendship between the clubs extending beyond the seating of the brand new Kyocera stadium. Local reporting spoke of their amazement as Swansea supporters mixed in with those from ADO, not a sight often seen in this part of the Hague. It made a colourful spectacle on an otherwise damp and dour game.

Swansea City haven't rested though, and Huw is pursuing all he can at Chelsea to secure Scott Sinclair on a transfer fee, not a loan. What I have found out is that Scott doesn't want a loan deal, he is sick of the insecurity of these deals having already spent long periods at too many clubs trying to settle. The obvious reason for this is the fact Chelsea want hard cash for him, and many of the clubs he has been at didn't have that type of money. He is still just a kid, aged twenty-one, and a real diamond. Come on Huw and Brendan, get the deal done, show some intent. He could really lift the Liberty this season – all he needs is that comforting feeling of being wanted, which Chelsea clearly cannot give him, neither could Wigan, very strange because with the right manager he will fly, I am sure of that.

Huw has now been badgered by the press so much he admits he is in talks with Chelsea about Scott Sinclair. It is no longer a secret, Huw – in fact it never was and hasn't been since Brendan arrived. I visit the bay that is Swansea and meet with a few friends and contacts to discuss our strategy for this book for the year. I don't want to upset anyone at the club and have no intention of engaging in character assassination on a whim, but this is an open forum as is anyone's life. So when a player gets me going, he should know about it. My gritty journey of Swansea self-realisation will be a long and expensive one. It will probably cost me over £5,000 this season. My accountant is aware and ready. It's a blustery mid-morning in Swansea as we gather for coffee in Mumbles having sought out too many beverages the night before. My acquaintances are already weary and looking forward to breakfast or, in one case, a long sleep. I have no desire to out my close friends, some who are more than very close to the board, we agreed a long time ago that our friendship would never interfere with their roles or jeopardise their positions. In fact I will go one stage closer, these people are 100 per cent Swansea City fans, they don't need their positions at Swansea City highlighted by me. However, our many years of friendship has always been our bond and the season is so close now that you can smell it. You can feel it breathing next to you, whispering its continual mantra, and the thousands who will make the journey north to Hull on Saturday know as well as I do that this is the first catalyst of the season, for the future of the club. It now feels strange that I won't be there for that opening gambit. Every moment, every decision will be a catalyst for Swansea City. Every fan, every journey, every fight, beer and friendship will be tested in a steely environment of cross-border hatred. We sense this as Swansea fans, even the very many English Jacks feel this resentment as well. They sense the hatred so much, the discontent and the utter poison directed towards us each and every away game. It is this finger-pointing lunacy that upstages common sense at every turn on our journey. It's them – the stinking Welsh, the contaminated classes. How dare they journey here, how dare they sing their songs when all we can do is wave sheep. They test us by waving, chanting, shouting, crying, laughing, joking, demanding and cultivating our responses. Those Welsh, those low-life scum from over there. The place we don't know about, the team that makes us wear our England jerseys because we believe it's an international fixture, when all it is – is Swansea. They speak funny, act funny, walk funny, shout funny, smell – weird. Are they so toxic that I must abuse them racially when they appear in my town? The Welsh. They don't like us and we don't like them. The English, we know they don't trust us, and trust them we do not. Tidy.

The fear of a new season and the rise in bilious content from the depths of my beer-stained gut are apparent as August marches towards the opening Saturday of the Championship season. I fear all sorts of things that will ruin my and many others' football year. Relegation and League One football are the greatest fear. This makes me feel sick after all the club has gone through. I have some reservations, too, about our Brendan. Is he really the right man for the job? I look at the squad and see straight away where we are deficient from a fan's point of view. I just hope from a manager's point of view Brendan sees them too.

Chapter Three

Holidays in the Sun

S tarting your season away at Hull City is never going to be easy. They have delusions of grandeur as to what league they should be in, and they have managers on gardening leave, most deluded – plus a new stadium, and a pretty healthy support as well. All of us love the first game of the season. That is, all of us apart from those who have other commitments. This may be lost on most of you, but will be of interest to a few. Every first weekend of August an event takes place in Blackpool called the Rebellion Festival, which if I am to be most truthful with you all, is one hell of a gathering. Maybe it's a bit more special as a one-off event than watching Swansea City? I can see Swansea play forty-six times a season if I want to. It isn't that often I get to see my real heroes of punk rock all under one roof. Yes, punk rock has gone all Butlins, and I love it.

The Swans have had a dodgy start, that's for sure, and couldn't survive what could well be the goal of the season from Hull City's John Bostock. I am told through blinkered eyes that the side were not that good, and failed miserably in the Humberside sunshine. The final score of 2–0 was about right, and if we expect to do anything this season then we need to strengthen up front. The same old Swansea City problem has arisen after 90 minutes of football – we need a striker, and it seems to most that Craig Beattie, due to countless injuries, is not the answer and neither is my man Stephen Dobbie. Not at the moment anyway. He needs more time. Much is expected of him, but I am not sure he is the answer at this stage of the season, maybe later, but not now. I also hear he may well have preferred a Blackpool switch before this season began; he has been quoted as saying as much. This striker assessment disappoints me. When we signed Craig I felt positive, but looking at the guy's stats for appearances for his age I was very surprised. He rarely played more than five games consecutively, and since arriving at Swansea has suffered already with countless injuries. For me he was a board signing when the manager, Paulo Sousa, had no idea or clue about who to bring in. Look at the agents' fees for the year, it tells a tale. I'm disappointed as I walk back into a hot but excited Winter Gardens – I have forty bands to choose from tonight on five stages, life could be worse. It could be a lot worse.

I find the start of the season a bit difficult to get involved in as a fan. There is the League Cup which rears its ugly head far too quickly. For me it could all be played over three or four weeks in January. This would allow clubs to field their experimental sides (think of that what you will – this is what clubs do, even Swansea) and will also allow a degree of recovery for those players who need it. I will say this as well, though, most clubs would end up in Dubai or similar places playing financially beneficial friendlies at some point, of that I have no doubt. A winter's break with the League Cup over a month I think would be a real goer. The fact the League Cup starts so early, and teams do go out of the competition in August means that the rewards are often not sighted by managers and players. Look at the faces of the players who have won a League Cup winners' medal in the final, and indeed the faces of the chairman and board when they realise they have a string of Europa Cup games to add to their financial balance sheets for the season. Look at Fulham – they benefited massively from their run to the 2010 Europa Cup final, defeating Juventus on the way. And Roy Hodgson gained as well, in being made manager of Liverpool. A strange appointment for me when you look at his track record . . . and with Kenny Dalglish desperate for the role it should have been a no-brainer of a decision. Too many no-brainers in football seems to be the problem sometimes.

The Swans have the opportunity to bounce back quickly and get the season up and running as a result of the League

Cup, so a home tie against Barnet should do the trick. Traditionally attendances are very small compared to league games for these early rounds and tonight is no different. I do like midweek games, but not those games where it's still light at the end. The woe of August again I am afraid. A weakened Swans side did over a Barnet team who I would describe as plucky, and maybe slightly unlucky early on in the second half. It has to be said, even though we have had a slippy start to the league season, this result was never in doubt, for all Barnet's efforts. Van der Gun, Pratley and Kuqi all end the Barnet dream, and a string of bookings at the end are evidence to the fact that it was full pelt to the final whistle. I dwell for a moment as I get into my car – could we win the League Cup? I say this because I feel that both Martinez and Sousa as managers failed to catch on to cup games, and the possibility of success. Both of them in the recent past have thrown away huge opportunities for the club to get financial reward, and for me as a fan they have failed to reward my support by making inappropriate team selections. I know there are arguments all round for this. Put quite clearly the issue is this: do we need to experiment or give players games just because we view the competition or opposition less favourably? Swansea City have lost a lot of money in recent years in doing this. Roberto Martinez threw away the chance of a game at Anfield in the FA Cup when he weakened the Swans for a replay game at Havant. And yes, we lost. I should imagine Huw and Co. were tamping.

Just as I think all is lost and we have a difficult season ahead in the league, up pop Preston North End. They have never fared well at Swansea in recent times, getting good thumpings on a regular basis. We often capitulate up there – it's as if we have a seasonal agreement between the two clubs. This is one of our more pivotal games. The reason will be clear once I get home from the game. If we lose then it could well be that league survival is our season's mission, if we win, and the manner of the win is important, it could be we have another chance of a tilt at the play-offs. Oh me of little faith.

The Besian tribute today was as moving as the football played by the Swans. PNE were battered out of sight; they looked very poor from the off and hardly threatened us. My man Dobbie scored as did Pratley, Dyer and Cotterill. I must say that after the game our journey home was sprinkled with talk of the win and the way it was achieved. The football oozed confidence across the park, and PNE looked like a team disorientated and desolate. The cry for a striker at the club may well die down now, but still there seems to be a need for a real number nine up front. Dobbie doesn't fit that bill – I think he needs a front man up there with him, to play-off him as we move forwards, and to link and move the structured and effective way we play. But then if we did, and went more four-four-two, would we have the best of the midfield game? I am immediately corrected by my travelling companion, one Kevin O' Brien, who states very clearly that we play a real attacking four-three-three and at times a three-seven! Kev has watched the Swans for years longer than I have – he can honestly remember the long shorts and tie-backed socks. That means he can also remember those desolate times of re-election, I can remember them too, but not as clearly. Kev's reflections of those days, and the effect on fans at the time, are far more ingrained on him than me. The attendances were indeed appalling, as was the football. For me, as a ten-year-old, they meant little, those cries of 'Swansea Aggro' from a windswept North Bank as we played our Division Four rivals. Long-haired louts in large boots with scarves tied around their wrists were the order of the day. Oxford bags, star jumpers, big collars and a waistband of three or even four buttons was the uniform. It was a time when knives were meant for knifing and guns were made to shoot, not that they did that much of either. Those words could well be prophetic today, but not then. And if the visitors should dare to score, a cry of 'You're gonna get your fucking heads kicked in' rang out from the massed faithful. 'You're going home in a Swansea ambulance' was another thread from the times, although the word 'Swansea' was sometimes replaced with 'black and white'. Now I know that should those daring braves from Doncaster or Walsall be injured enough to need an ambulance, it wouldn't be a Swansea one that took them home. In fact did anyone go home in an ambulance? Would it not be your mum or dad who picked you up?

When at our old stamping ground of the Vetch Field, a visiting supporter was not a good thing to be. Since I first stepped on to those broad North Bank steps I have always sensed mischief among the natives. Most games saw the crew of the day run round the outskirts of the ground to meet head-on the opposition that dared to walk the Swansea streets – Swansea boot boys of old gearing up for new trends just around the corner, like punk rock and skinhead stardom, their cries far different to those of today. The reason, I believe, is that the numbers were bigger. The opposition were more often than not less happy to involve themselves in such conflict at the magical time of 4.40 p.m., no longer as brave as they were when a football field apart. The lure of the sea would become the stuff of Swansea legend in later years, but let me tell you now that first recorded sortie into Swansea Bay by Cardiff fans was not actually the first event of its kind. Many went before them, better swimmers they were as well, so I am told.

Swansea City rarely sought re-election off the field.

I get home to Gloucester in record time, on the crest of a Swansea wave, with other Jacks passing us and then us passing them on the motorway, expressing our only joyous link, that is our team as a connection. Thumbs up, horns sounding, the fast lane attack. It's amazing how many Swans fans turn off at Pencoed, Bridgend and Cardiff after a game. It really does put to bed the theory that our support is more West Wales-based than Cardiff-based.

I remember a time when we were bottom of the league, cannon fodder, only threatening to get promoted. Those days threw together a well-organised support from the West Country, and at times a full bus from Gloucestershire alone. There were end-of-season dinners with certain players – indeed, one evening with Jan Molby, who was our guest in front of 150 Swansea supporters in the city of Gloucester, lives long in the memory. I am not surprised the owners of old shivered in their expensive suits at the mobilisation of such a passionate support, and so far away. Thinking back now we could have done so much more, but camaraderie was our only cause. I wonder if the new supporters' board felt as threatened as those of old did when they took over in 2002? I wonder. But I remember much, and have the odd bit of mending to do myself. On behalf of others we act, and for the common good we react. Even years later.

Chapter Four

Autumnal Rain

Swansea City spend a lot of time under the radar. The bleeping green screen of football's hierarchy will ignore the club as will those who do not venture as far west as others. The ignorance of those attached to the media and other football bodies know little if anything of the club, its fans and players. Even some football fans have failed in recent times to understand the city's location as regards the rest of the world. When the club played Scunthorpe United in an ill-fated play-off semi-final in 1999 Scunny's fans left their Lincolnshire base at 6 a.m. for the journey to Swansea. They arrived at 9.30ish and wandered about waiting for the city to wake up. Speaking to some who arrived by minibus, they thought the journey would take some five or six hours, maybe even seven. I smiled, and left them to ponder the grey, overcast Swansea skyline. I mean a real Scunthorpe supporter would know the journey time. That would be those who arrived in good time some hours later, a more acceptable time for the game perhaps. Not at the crack of dawn!

Big games encourage all sorts of bandits and non-entities to surface in their club's colours – one-game-a-season fans. I question at times if these people are of any use to a club and its future. They disappear as quickly as they turn up. Fraudulently purporting to be a fan, like Northampton Town's 40,000 turn-out at Wembley two years earlier in 1997, I put the majority in the pure simpletons bracket. The arrogance that oozed out of some of them was unbelievable. I even tried to talk to one guy as I left the toilets close to Wembley Way. He sounded like he knew everything, mistaking me for someone who was just like him maybe? His racist rhetoric about sheep and Welsh people was a disgusting parody of a selfish, nasty little man with nothing. I later saw him bloodied and injured, complaining and shouting at two police officers. I also saw John Hartson that day, he was wearing big cowboy boots with a bag of chips in his hand laughing and enjoying the day with his mates. A different football picture, an honest portrayal of what the day should have been about. Yes we are ignored at Swansea City by most, hated by many, and after such a long time of knowing that this is the case – we quite enjoy it.

The Swansea City desire for a red-hot striker continues as well. Pitman at Bournemouth is linked but I already know he is pretty much tied in to a deal at Bristol City, and more interestingly we have Frank Nouble touted as a possibility. Frank could well fit the bill, but he is very young, and his loans to date from West Ham have not been brilliantly successful. I suppose for a kid of such tender years he has done okay? I'm not sure about this one.

The Swans get Tranmere away in the League Cup, another battling performance will be required up there to get anything at all. I see this as further ammo to my cause of a solid three weeks to settle the tournament. I have to make mention of this – I wasn't going to – but as the month cracks on Cardiff City have been well up there in the headlines. I'm not sure if August brings with it sprinklings of madness like March, but Cardiff City have signed Craig Bellamy. Regardless of the cost, the logistics or the doubts (and when it comes to Cardiff City there have to be doubts), this is one hell of a signing. Even if he only plays twenty games.

The wheels will always be wobbly at this time of the season and this is the case after dominating matters at Norwich City. Carrow Road is not the best of hunting grounds for us, although Ferrie Bodde's goal a few seasons back was worth the three points alone. David Cotterill misses a penalty and we succumb to some last-minute madness to lose the game 2–0. Brendan isn't happy after dominating such a great part of a decent game of football, and even I can see that our league position will improve if we carry on playing this way. Norwich manager Paul Lambert agrees – he believes Swansea play football the right way. Well, I suppose for him and Norwich we do, the defeat is hard to take.

It is clear we do need a bit of inspiration, Scott Sinclair is yet to catch fire, he promises so much but so far there is no cigar for the young man. Another young man in our sights is Henri Lansbury. Now I do like this player – a lot. He is an Arsenal product who would really make a difference to us in the midfield and when going forward. But he does earn a wedge at Arsenal – wages which I am sure we can't match. These deals can be done between the clubs quite easily, although it does depend on what the parent club want to receive for the player, but in Arsenal's case it sometimes isn't huge amounts of money. Traditionally it's a third of the player's wage, but these deals do fluctuate and I get the impression Swansea are stalling, their decision-making not as effective as it could be with regards to Henri. It could well be the board don't fancy him, but then the manager's relationship with them I know is sound, so it maybe isn't a disagreement on that front. I'm thinking it's more the money side of things . . . we shall see. Brendan may be impressed with the Swansea City set-up, but the controllers of the club's future are precious about what they have achieved, and the manager has not done anything to really inspire absolute confidence yet. Maybe a League Cup run will release the purse strings?

Avoiding my usual travelling companions I attend the Tranmere League Cup game with a gracious fellow, a man who you will often see on the television on a Saturday night spilling forth his excellent point of view on the Championship. I will keep his identity for now, in fact I see no reason to disclose his name. Suffice to say, he's driving and tonight I get to see the game from the other side of the pitch. Someone else I speak to now and then is ex-Premier League referee Clive Wilkes, a very decent chap who I will freely admit I rated as an abject lunatic after a Bristol Rovers away game many years ago in Bath. That day he sent off Carl Heggs and Stephen Torpey, and cost us the game. In fact, knowing what I know now I am aware it was the players who cost us the game, Clive was merely the catalyst for them leaving pitch. A genuinely nice guy and quality reader of the game, he now assesses referees and I really have to take up his offer of a game or two from the referee's point of view before this season ends. Maybe.

See – it's not what you know, it *is* who you know in this game. Unlike Clive I am not the subject of media gagging orders. He is currently fighting his ageism and unfair dismissal case in the courts along with Paul Durkin (he of the staggering backwards crazy dance, Di Canio-style with tuck) and various other assembled referees. And being one who identifies with causes that are clearly just and with foundation, I support him 100 per cent. It will rumble on and on I am sure. But there is no way you should be removed from the theatre of conflict if you are fit, able and, most importantly, experienced. Clive is all those things, and the football law-makers need taking to task as much as they can be. Just because you are in a position of trust doesn't make you a law-maker, because for every law-maker there is a law-breaker.

Tranmere is dismal though, not that I dislike the place, it just feels lost in a sphere of no hope. Complicated roads and industrial pasts count for nothing in the League Cup though. I mean they do have the illustriously named Enoch Showunmi, and even better squad names like Cathalina and Bakayogo; it doesn't get much better than this in the Wirral. I am certain I saw Andy Robinson on the way in, I would have said hello, but I didn't want to. I'm firmly fixed on the game, this could be a watershed for Swansea City, one of many weekly watersheds we will have before we enter May 2011 and the final month of the season. At this time this is a cup game, it figures nowhere in the league campaign. We could win the thing and go down – that's football for you.

Brendan fields a relatively decent side which tells me he is desperate to make a mark on this cup competition and indeed with the board. A loss here isn't the end of the world, but he knows more than anyone that a manager's job is the most shaky of all appointments. It may pay well but it sometimes doesn't pay well for long. His experience at Reading would have taught him that. When the Swans go one down to a goal from Showunmi, I get agitated, and my celebrity mate urges caution as the 2,450 crowd cheer the opener for Tranmere. When I say 2,450, I should give the travelling Swans support a mention, noisy and passionate throughout the game, and numbering a decent 400 or so I would say. I am not that good at counting people, if I was I would be in charge of the national census, so I apologise for any misreporting of the total. By half time I am very concerned that Brendan's arms are beginning to fold and this, in a Jan Molby type of way, signals a pondering man in a difficult situation.

I also have to say at this point that the Swans did play reasonably well, but not emphatically well. And although the end result did go in our favour, it was only after Dobbie and Sinclair came on, and only then after seventy minutes of huff and puff. The three Swansea goals for me clouded a questionable performance, and as it was Dobbie and Sinclair who scored two of the three goals I feel I have a point. Cedric van der Gun got the other, a player who is clearly on the periphery of Brendan's thinking this season. The aggression shown tonight was pleasing to see in the second half, but Tranmere for me are a team who will struggle in League One this time around, and Swansea have much to do. The third round beckons though, and we all dream of that big, big draw.

As we speed along the pretty empty motorways back to Gloucester it is announced that George Rockwell Lincoln died on this day in 1967 in the USA. 'Thank heavens for that,' my mate responds, 'I thought he was crap in midfield for most of his career.' George was many things, but centre midfield he was not.

Stephen Dobbie signed a new deal with Swansea today, and after all his previous indications of wanting to join Blackpool, I am happy to read that he has done so. He must sense a revolution happening at Swansea City, I sort of do as well, and as I mooch around the sweetcorn in my garden after an evening in the north-west I begin to feel a bit more positive. I have to be careful at times, I do get the nod on these things before they happen from time to time, like we all do – I have my sources. However, I read this in the paper, so I am not jeopardising anyone for this revelation. I have been told that my Swansea book will cause some stirring in the city itself, but reading through it this morning I can't see how. Am I being judged on the person I was when I was angry and ready for a war? Nowadays, as I keep having to say, I am at peace with the club I support, the people who run matters and the staff that wear the shirt. Well, for now. I will always keep an eye on it, though . . . so maybe that's the problem?

When you are a football maniac you can go from complete highs to absolute rock-bottom in one go. One minute everything in the garden is rosy, the next a dark cloud descends and releases a bile-like rotten lump of vomit all over your endives. Then it rains, and I can smell that vomit again. These highs and lows are all a part of football fandom. But I really do hate feeling sick and happy all at once.

Things will always be put into perspective by the plight of others. I am saddened to read that Alan Tate, described as a Swans legend, has many family problems. His dad has just had a second bowel cancer operation, and this saddens me further. Tate senior has been a constant supporter of his son since he joined from Manchester United. I have spoken to him on a number of occasions, he oozes pride for his son, and I can understand why. He is a decent bloke. Tatey could have walked away a few years ago when he wasn't anywhere near the side under previous managers. But his resolute performance (in goal no less) v QPR a few seasons back confirmed to many his 'legendary status'. Now as you know, for me there shouldn't be legends or individual praise for this very well paid job. However, in Tatey's case there is much praise for him as a person, and an ambassador of Swansea City. I remember his dad's excitement after we defeated Rochdale way back in 2003 as we scraped ourselves towards league safety. Bill was absolutely ecstatic, and it was etched all over his face. He was so proud of what had been achieved and he certainly looked like the proudest dad in Manchester that day.

It's the end of the month and we are all up for a home game against Burnley – always a tough side to get a result from. Today will be no different. It's still pretty hot and this suits our football I think. The Brazilian format is still the template for the Arsenalesque style of play. See, I'm just brimming with confidence again! It's sunny, and the Swans are going to fly today, I just know it. Rossi's chippy is packed – always a good sign of a big crowd – and the rissoles are in fine fettle. The Globe public house is also visited and a few real ales downed – well, just because it's a football must. This all signals a jolly decent end-of-day result. There are games when you just know you will win, and this, my friends, is the case today. It is far too sunny for it not to be.

Burnley don't see it that way though and Tyrone Mears means business. He will let no man pass. Mears and Darren Pratley are treated to an early bath. Maybe both sendings off could have been better managed by referee Steve Tanner, whom incidentally, Harry Redknapp once described as 'scary'. I would describe him as 'jumpy'. Why do refs not wait those few seconds before stopping the game. Our free-flowing style wasn't stopped that much by the Burnley defence, indeed it was more so by referee Tanner's whistle. Do I really want to pay my hard-earned cash to see the ref? He dished out a staggering six yellows today and two reds. His record is complete madness. He goes from a careful-thinking referee to one who is overcome with the desire to dole out as many cards as he can. Take this on board folks – last season Steve Tanner refereed thirty-four games. He booked 111 players and sent off nine in those games. 111 players in thirty-four games? Yes, that's right. Spot on. I can't work that out, and looking at his stats neither could the eight players he booked at Watford v WBA either.

Not even Steve Tanner can take away the joy of this result, it is a kick-start to an indifferent month. The 1–0 victory, secured by Scott Sinclair could (and should) have been more, and even Brian Laws was forced to agree that his team was second class at all levels. Not before he blamed

Mears, though, for the loss. He's a mad egg is he not? I'll give him three months max.

Henri Lansbury seems no closer to signing for Swansea, it's deadline day and among all the rumours I can only see Kemy Agustien being added to the squad. Sinclair has cost a decent wedge by Swansea standards, and with wage increases this could be all the business we do. Leroy Lita, Danny Graham and Tamas Priskin are all linked and fade away. I don't fancy any of them with the exception of Graham – he seems to be working well at Watford. There is always the feeling he could well be a one- or two-season wonder, but looking at him and talking to a few well-placed scouts, I know the belief is he could well be the real deal this season. Watford want money though, and Swansea rarely splash out more than twice a year on big fees. It's the way, and for some of us it's the right way. Then all of a sudden we get Frank Nouble-d and the big man is rumoured to have arrived on the shores of Swansea Bay . . . albeit on loan. Will he be the answer to our goalscoring problems? No, because it didn't happen, sometimes it's who you know that annoys me most!

After the deadline-day deals are done Swansea disclose that Celtic and Leicester made fairly decent offers for Ashley Williams. I knew of Leicester City's interest, and I knew they would be prepared to offer £2 million or so for him, so I was happy that would be put to bed sooner rather than later. I sense that Paulo is getting desperate already in the crisps stadium. There is no way that Ash will be leaving for that amount of money. However, it is Celtic that make me laugh. They ask how much we want – they are told £4 million and that's the end of that. As far as I am concerned we undervalued him. In *Fawlty Towers*' Mrs Richards style they should have been told '£5 million and not a penny less'. Ashley is a quality centre-half, and an excellent player, if not one of the Championship's best. Why League One-standard Celtic would find the fee so offputting amazes me. He would enhance them immediately, and enhance his own rat-catching skills as well. He's a dab hand, our Ash.

Brendan Rodgers has gained some confidence after the Burnley win; he looks a bit more positive in press calls, and is beginning to stamp his own character on the club. This starts with him referencing, and not for the first time, Ferrie Bodde in the press. It's early September and owing to the international break and no league games there is little news about. The deadline transfers are done and dusted, so I sense a bit of meddling by the press here. They cite Brendan as wanting Bodde back in Wales to monitor his rehabilitation – meddling with his words methinks. The Swansea story this season must not be a positive one in the national or local press of Wales – that is one line of thought, while others are not so full of conspiracy. My mind is not made up, not yet. In fact it is, at times the press in Wales can be a little one-sided when it comes to Cardiff City. This is because many of their Cardiff-based reporters are Cardiff City fans. It's not rocket science – that's for the likes of Howard from Cowbridge to sort out. This is far simpler, like some of the decision-making of certain Swansea players of recent seasons, this is a no-brainer. I would be the same you know.

I'm not that bothered about international matches. I lost interest after a seven-goal drubbing in Holland some years ago. I will skim over whatever fare is on offer this week and look forward to our next game . . . it can't be that far away. I'm at a loss to be honest, not totally, but nearly. Brendan is happy with his lot at Swansea, and seeing as this is his very first full season as a manager (we hope), he is doing well, and I am sure he would agree with me. The Swansea model is a simple one: don't lose money, don't put the club anywhere near where we were in 2002 and 2003, and gently push forward having gained simple ground doing so. The problem is we do have the odd bogey side away from home and Leeds are fast becoming one of those sides. We seem to talk the talk when we play them at Elland Road but unfortunately that is all that happens. The squad this time around are more prepared than the last visit, when we lost, and utter mayhem ensued outside the ground. So I am hopeful that today we will put them away in good style. The big difference for me is players like Neil Taylor who are slowly gaining a footing at a much higher level and not looking out of place. He says so himself: 'I'm just living the dream,' he states in the press. Well Neil me old mucker, I'm living the dream as well, especially now that you are too. Nice one.

Leeds next then, and the game, like our recent visits, starts brightly enough but sadly disappears into the dust as they deservedly win 2–1. Is it the fact that Elland Road has housed so many legendary players over the years – admittedly not recently – but is that the reason? I mean, after Dobbie slammed us in front I really felt this was our day. Another second-half capitulation. We're not ready to go the full ninety is the problem at the moment. Even Ian Snodin's comment, that he sees no weaknesses in the Swansea side, holds little comfort – there are a few, and it seems mental toughness is one of them. We are settling for a result too early, and this is causing us to fold as pressure is put on the back four. That's my assessment today, it may not count for much, but it's getting costly, albeit if this is only our second away defeat of the season. I see more like this, and that is slightly worrying. The Swans are fourteenth in a Championship that is very competitive. I've poured a few short ones, salvaged a few thoughts and wonder what all the fuss is about. It's not that bad.

Chapter Five

Big Frank is a Bit Leggy

Well, QPR are top. I expected that, Cardiff are second – that too is no surprise. In the Championship, what in time I am sure will be the key is that no matter who plays who and when, any side can win. And that gives us a chance on a very level playing field. I suppose the real shocker after five league games is that Portsmouth are bottom, and looking already like they are dead and buried. Forty-one games to go though, and as ever I reckon if this is a season of survival then we'd better get to fifty points quickly. This league is wide, wide open.

The nice thing about the Championship is that because of all the international botheration, if you happen to lose on a Saturday then when Tuesday comes it can be put right. This time around we have Coventry City and their magnificent away support at the Liberty. Star-spangled light blue chaps in a swish away kit of – I don't know what you would call it really. More interestingly I get a phone call in the afternoon stating that Shefki Kuqi is on his way to Derby County. For some reason his three-minute bursts of enthusiasm are not required this side of Christmas at the Liberty. Some do seem to like him though and I do admire his sudden bursts of energy. My view is that if you play him forty-six times, if fit, he will get you twenty goals. Unlike poor old Gorka Pintado who I am also hearing is thinking of playing his last few seasons in football elsewhere. He just needs to find someone, anyone, who will take him. Kuqi will always find a club, but surely he should be looking down the leagues rather than up?

Coventry City under floodlights look slick and well-positioned to give us a good old game, that's for sure. Darren Pratley settles us all down with a pretty classy header and Scott Sinclair made the best of what I can only describe as an awful back-pass just as the second half got under way. Then we did it again. I am now angry – again. We decided to protect what we had with no idea of how this could be achieved. Granted Nathan missed a couple of chances, but once again he was magnificent, and then some bloke called Turner, turned us all upside down to make it 2–1. In true *Dad's Army* style Swansea are doing the 'Don't panic' waltz as they try their very best to gift Coventry a point. Maybe it's because Coventry haven't won at Swansea since 1950 or something that we feel the need to at least give them a lifeline. Monk clears off the line and again I will give the lad some grace – Nathan Dyer really should have buried them out of sight but their keeper did well to keep the effort out. Overall it was a deserved victory, and again I find myself asking the question, 'Am I asking too much?' I probably am, but that's the way of the football fan. I do know though that even if this fixture was a non-league match in front of 200 at home, I would be one of those hardy souls. It's in the blood see, mush? Coventry are despatched back to the Ricoh and their 200 or so supporters who looked like they were watching death wake up went home as well. Except one brave soul who calmly reflected on the game in the Coopers. Yes, a Welsh Coventry City fan from Townhill no less. How the mind boggles.

We go flying up the league one place to thirteenth. Leap-frogging Coventry on the way – effectively a six-pointer. QPR's win at Ipswich is worrying, they seem unstoppable and a 3–0 win at Portman Road is a great result. I like Warnock as well, mental chap that he is. He seems as mad as a hatter – but is he really? Or is he just a passionate football man, who loves football things? I think he is the latter. In any event, QPR are looking red-hot, and as my good mate Marcus from Merthyr rings to tell me – 'We are dead certs for the up mush, let me tell you Keith, the

Rs are going up.' I reckon he needs a spell in the foreign legion. Paulo's Leicester beat Cardiff, so a few smiles there, but result of the night has to be Scunthorpe's 4–0 drubbing of Leon Britton's Sheffield United, I wonder how he feels tonight?

I've got to remind you of Aidy Boothroyd's quote after the game before we put this one to bed. He cleverly looks into the camera, steadies himself and says 'It was a game of two halves.' Nice one Aidy, and once again what was it? 'A game of two halves.' Really, you do impress me. He is a good mate of Brendan's but I hope he doesn't spend too much time with him on those long dark winter nights ahead.

We have replaced Kuqi with a Frank Nouble. He's a big Bruno-type striker from West Ham. A young lad indeed, and with one or two attributes in front of goal that may well help as the Swansea tank moves slowly forwards. Frank is another ex-Chelsea player who Brendan rates highly and he cites the player making his debut at sixteen when he was first a reserve-team player at Stamford Bridge. No mean feat that, and after the change in Scott Sinclair's fortunes already this season who am I to grumble? Then it all goes Marc Clode when Avram Grant is quoted as saying 'Frank is a very good player, I rate him highly.' Now I have my doubts. I'll make a judgement here. Avram will fall off his perch at West Ham even quicker than the leaves on my trees. Either that or he will take them down to our hard-fought and very difficult league. I bet they lose a few when that happens, and I don't mean grey hairs. I've seen Frank in the flesh, he isn't that big, but he looks a powerful unit. You never know. Let's leave it at that.

It's the Swansea way that at least four times a season we play a team that have just lost their manager. In this case it's Scunny who beat Sheffield United 4–0 away a few days ago. The nice thing though, is that this game is at home and Scunthorpe don't fare that well against us, either home or away. Somebody else who is beginning to really impress me is Mark Gower. I am sure he will forgive me for saying this but he was absolutely awful at times last season; now there is one hell of a transformation taking place in him. It's worth noting how much more involved he is now, and how well he is playing. He seems in control, in focus and – in position. His previous stints out on the wings have not done his confidence any good at all. But now in a more holding role in the centre of midfield and deep, he is like a man reborn. I am really pleased for him, and for us. He is currently most definitely like a new signing. I hope he can keep his form in place, because for me at this time he is the link between a very ball-possessive defence and midfield. It's a remarkable turnaround.

Scunthorpe are despatched very much in the same way as they are always despatched at home, convincingly. I will say this, though, they took the edge out of the game well and it took another effort from Scott Sinclair and a great strike from Dobbie to seal it. They made us work really hard for the ball, and the journey home was an interesting one with my travel buddies really looking upwards as opposed to downwards in the league. I have made notes today as well, so I can explain to you more about what I saw. However, a game is a game, and we won. You won't bother too much, I know, if I leave it at that. Oh, apart from one thing. Kev from Henley has given up cricket. The godfather of Henley-in-Arden has hung up his bat and will continue in retirement – as a retired cricketer. It's sad really, he looked like he had another over in him. I reckon he won't be able to drag himself right away from the willow and ball thing. I can see him now making the butties and working behind the bar.

The league table becomes more interesting after four consecutive home wins. The Leeds game is now a dim and distant (albeit only seven-day-old) memory and in the interim we have gained six good home points from two games against tough opponents. We are sixth in the table. This time of the season odd things like this happen. Swansea City in a play-off place, eh? Can we stop now? I would like to get off. Looking around us QPR are still top with Watford in the mix, and above us are Norwich

– a surprise? Then there's that lot up the road. Ipswich have gained momentum too, and are my brother's tip for promotion. Personally I think he is mad. However, after seven league games they are second.

Brendan brings us all down to earth again, though. As soon as a team gets into the top six the inevitable questions start, and he explains directly that although we are there it is difficult to say we are promotion contenders. This is purely due to the amount of money the other clubs in the league have at their disposal. He is right, but I will say this, I don't care what he says about league tables and results. I know full well, as we all do, that when he sips his Horlicks of an evening, that he will be checking Ceefax and scanning that Championship table like he has never done before. Because like us, he is a fan, and he knows that in football fairytales do come true, maybe not yet – but they do. My reckoning is that if he gets us anywhere near the play-offs he will easily secure himself another season, because this season, being our third in the Championship, can only be improved upon by getting into the play-offs. With what we have at our disposal he is right, it is a very tall order indeed. Brendan's first season with us is going to get interesting as the weather gets colder.

Coming up next we have Forest away and Watford away. I hate going to Forest, so I won't bother. My theory here is that my being present won't do anything to enhance matters, and every time I do go it's a shit day out. I will level with you, they are a big club, they won two European Cups you know, but I don't need to hear it every three minutes in a stupid accent, and I don't need them taunting me as I leave the ground with another victory or dodgy draw. We all have teams we don't like, and Forest are one for me. Newcastle are another, they hardly welcome you to their neck of the woods with open arms. And then they moan when the same type of hospitality is afforded them when they come to Swansea. You can't have it both ways boys and girls. I would rather a good old drink up and a bit of banter followed by a game of football; seemingly there are those still following football who don't.

So, I don't like Forest – or Notts Forest as I like to call them. They know what I mean. I won't go to Watford either – some fan I am.

Chapter Six

Wig Wam Bam

Midweek Carling Cup games have never bothered me, not even when they look like they might be interesting. I will now introduce you to another team I don't like – Peterborough United. Remember, this is in football fandom terms. In reality I love the place, great chips, nice pint and a smashing link road which means you can avoid it completely. I find their persistent flag-bearer – one Adrian Durham – totally annoying on Talksport for 90 per cent of the time, although now and again he does make sense. I have a theory here. If you banged your gums together for three hours constantly every day for five days a week without drawing breath, at some point you will make sense as well.

People at football . . . it all gets very emotive. I recall a steward at Peterborough who blatantly baited the Swansea fans, gesturing and mouthing obscenities. He was a horrible fat man in a fluorescent coat. Then, all of a sudden, I couldn't see him, he was gone. About five minutes later I saw a big fat bloke being carried away on a stretcher. I later found out he had been given a bop on the nose. We all have to take the rough with the smooth, my friend. But the occasion and the atmosphere clearly got to him. I want to go to the game – then I change my mind and stay at home, I have my hair to wash and nails to do. I am glad I did too: it was a cake walk, a mere stroll in the park. Simple as that. Durham, your team are pants. Scott Sinclair 3 The Posh 1. Goodnight.

The footnote to this game is Garry Johnson, the Peterborough oddball manager, claiming they should have had five penalties. Yeah right mate, and you, Mr Johnson, are clutching at straws, especially the one you're chewing on.

The draw for the next round is made on Saturday, when we officially will get another rubbish draw no doubt. We don't get the Arsenals away and the Chelseas away like our friends in Cardiff. We get Barnet, Tranmere and Peterborough. Nearly as hard as Cardiff's FA Cup run to Wembley. Frank Nouble is in Brendan's thoughts for Forest, as he states we have managed to settle our goalscoring issues with three good strikers to choose from. I remain unconvinced as yet.

While the hardy 1,200 made the Forest trip I settled down to watch the Carling Cup draw. Lo and behold and let there be light . . . we get a Premier League team. And not just any Premier League team. We get Wigan Athletic. In normal terms one could see it as a bit of a let-down, but in our terms their manager is one Roberto Martinez. This could be a right cracker.

This all unfolds as Forest do the dirty on us again and soundly beat us 3–1. They are looking a good bet for this year. I just hope we can avoid them if this league does take us into the top six. Today we don't look anything like a top six side, mercilessly beaten in Nottinghamshire by Notts Forest.

More of a concern is that we as a team have not recorded an away win for six months, that's relegation form in my book. Okay, there has been a close-season in between, but it's eight in a row by my reckoning. There are glimpses of the free-flowing football we have seen at the Liberty, but really only glimpses. I am not too concerned, Craig Beattie may well be, though. Roy is Keane on him at Portman Road. Brendan seems Kean-o to shift him as well. He is even ringing Mad Roy to get him to make a decision. Careful Brendan, he'll set his dogs on you and go all strange.

The poor result at Forest sends us down to ninth and them into eleventh. QPR win again. This is getting familiar. They despatch Doncaster with ease at their place. Cardiff beat Millwall in the vile derby 2–1, and Portsmouth hammer Leicester 6–1 at Fratton Park, the two sides occupying the bottom two meeting head to head. I reckon Paulo could be in a tricky situation if he keeps eating too many crisps.

We have to focus though, because thanks to the Football League computer, once again we are away in midweek, this time at Watford. They are one of Brendan's old teams. He did well there but left to go to Reading, so I wonder what sort of reception he will get?

So Swansea City's away form has been poor, but I think Watford are the type of side that we can get something from. Eight away defeats on the bounce have to come to an end sometime. It's a bit wet tonight, and it's clear the winter is beginning to give us a nudge. Watford is achievable and achieved it is in two hours. I decide to do this one alone for the purposes of writing this book. I want to be able to watch and learn without interruption. I know my travelling companions will understand. It's nice as well, because I can hang around a few people in the know as it were. I get a nose in straight away and hear that Paulo has been told he has to win tonight or he's off. Not surprising really, as Leicester expect a little bit more this season than relegation.

Brendan's desire to win is matched by Swansea's desire on the pitch – no matter what he says he will want this one badly. Scott Sinclair, who is turning into the signing of any season, gets a goal, as does Stephen Dobbie. Even Frank Nouble weighs in with a quarter-pound hammer blow to give the Swans a 3–0 lead. This was easy, and as this was the last place at which the Swans had won on the road, a fitting recharge to the season. Every fan will know, though, that when a home side, even when three down, gets a sniff they can be very dangerous. Watford pull one back but it's no big deal as we have ten minutes to go. But then they weigh in with another. Oh dear, this is tricky. Then they have a goal disallowed. It looked okay to me, too. The Watford fans roar their side on, and I have to be clear here, if they were us I would have been gutted. But fortune favours the brave and we hold on for all three points. The travelling thousand-plus are delighted. I am delighted and the boos ring out around the ground. They are for the referee, Brendan, and probably us as well. Not to worry, it could be worse. You could be Luton. We controlled the flow for much of the game, but at last we got some reward for our total football style. It may work if we persevere, or it could well just Doncaster us completely. I'm not sure about Albert Serran though, he doesn't get enough game time for me to feel in control of all that goes on around him. Nathan Dyer, on the other hand, is blossoming at the moment. He has gone from terrier to tornado. I'm not sure if he knows what his legs will do next but in the crazy world of Nathan Dyer, I don't care. He is a magnificent, tireless team player.

Swansea City are eighth tonight. QPR draw in the London derby in Shepherd's Bush against Millwall and Preston win 6–4 at Leeds. Incredible stuff, and for Paulo I fear it is over. His Leicester lose at Norwich 4–3. What a night for goals. The top of the table reads QPR, Cardiff, Norwich, Watford, Burnley, Reading, Ipswich and Swansea. Happy days.

Brendan is still tinkering with the team. He has Ashley Williams in midfield at the moment, and I am not sure why. Serran at the back doesn't fill me with confidence, but up front we do seem to be getting it right. Frank Nouble's goal will do him the world of good. He is young and needs confidence. He also states he wants to leave Swansea with everyone talking about him when his loan finishes. That gets my mind racing, what has he been up to?

My information on Paulo is spot on. He did mention once that he likes golf . . . well he can go and watch the Ryder Cup in Newport now because Milan Mandaric has sacked him. Never one to be backwards in coming forwards he gives old Paulo the boot. The grass is never greener after Swansea, Paulo – many have found out this way before, and probably a few will this season as well, if not at the end. Mandaric reminds me of a cold war spy, sneaking quietly into position as his poison-tipped brolly is poised to strike out at you in your local bus shelter. Mandaric strikes and you're dead, a big heap on the floor.

At last a home game and our happy band speeds west again for the visit of Derby County. It's a really good opportunity to wipe the smiles off a few faces. We did them fairly easy last season, with Robbie Savage in shock as the winner hit the back of the net. His fault as well, I reckon. His backside-showing antics of last season to the Swansea East Stand will no doubt be repeated. Bending down for an extremely long period of time in front of the crowd while warming up, is an invitation, I reckon, to boot him right in the arse. However, a three-year ban is not what I want, plus all the hassle that goes with it. For some reason Swansea supporters hate him, really detest the bloke. I don't understand why, and then I hear him on the radio, and quickly realise exactly why. He is a wind-up merchant, and he is from North Wales. Not a bad thing, but it brings out the worst in people, you understand. When I was writing Roger Freestone's book I met up with John Hartson and Phil Sumbler at the Vale Hotel. I saw Robbie Savage standing outside the hotel in a tracksuit. I'm not joking he looked so effeminate, long hair and all, that I gave him a second glance. I wouldn't like – you obviously know that – but to me for that moment he looked like a dodgy blond hanging around outside the Wales international squad looking for a husband. He is a character is Robbie Savage, but then so is Lily Savage. He loves the banter and to wind up the crowd. Literally every time he comes to Swansea he goes through the ritual of bending down in front of the East Stand for longer than necessary. It really gets everyone going – not the sight of his backside – but his sheer arrogance. Football thrives on it.

We have some deficiencies today, no Darren Pratley and in particular no Scott Sinclair. So we get to see Andrea Orlandi – he who wanted away in the summer – and Cedric van der Gun, who can score a decent goal or two. The bench has Jordi Lopez on it as well, a player who Sousa felt would turn us around last season and then never really gave him a chance. He is on a few quid as well, which must infuriate the chairman. Especially a chairman who has presided over financial matters so carefully. You get talked into buying a player, a decent wedge is agreed in wages and then he doesn't do anything but warm a bench seat with his backside. The same could be said about Craig Beattie, a most infuriating player, more effort always seems to result in an injury.

From the off it is clear that Nigel Clough, the Derby manager, has come to do a job on us. He is learning, very slowly, but he is learning. Last season we did a credible double on them, but this time it is going to be a lot harder. A tightly packed defence was hitting our weakened side on the break – a worrying trend. Nathan Dyer seemed quiet, and van der Gun, pretty much as expected, was lacking in guile, pace and know-how. I really wanted him to do well too. Scott Sinclair he was not. Joe Allen had been partnered with Orlandi, and that clearly wasn't working. Orlandi was trying, but he was trying in a League One sort of way. Sadly, being the corner-taker and potential free-kick-taker wasn't doing it for me. He seems lightweight and, although skilful, he was clearly out of this depth. This was having an impact across the team as Derby got more courageous and more direct. Joe Allen seemed to fall apart at times, off the pace and off the park would probably be the best move for young Joe. The game then seemed to gently move towards a quiet and frustrating climax. Garry Monk looked nowhere near his best which allowed Derby to nearly secure all the points and it was only Dobbie who threatened briefly. My word, what a frustrating day. A nailed-on three points ends up as just one. No red cards and no yellow cards tells more of a tale than I could. I do have another one of my theories though: because we were so weakened and then introduced Beattie, Orlandi and Lopez it clearly indicates that our strength in depth is not as good as we thought this season. Brendan will know this if I do. What he can do about it? Indeed what is he allowed to do about it given his financial constraints? This is why he wants players out, so he can get players in.

Oh and Savage obliged this afternoon with his customary backside display. It received many cheers, jeers and laughter all around. Oh what a jolly jape.

The journey home was a bit downbeat. I see it like this. It was another point gained to stay up and retain our Championship status. You can talk all you like about our ability and passing game. But for now, it's about getting to fifty points as quickly as possible. Survival is the key. Other results in the league today see Cardiff win at Barnsley and yes, you guessed it, QPR win at Palace. Leicester City players send Paulo a message in his absence and win at home against Scunthorpe lifting them to third bottom. We are eighth. Nice.

At home that night, reflecting on Brendan's appointment and the players he has at his disposal, I suppose his school report would read along these lines:

> 'Brendan has a flair for organisation and team bonding. With the players he has, he is operating above average. This is illustrated by his current position of eighth in the class. Other boys have tried to cause Brendan some issues by bullying him, but he has his own mind and once made up seems to want to carry it through to the end. It's almost as if he is proving himself to someone. He may be small, but Brendan is developing a loud voice – he needs to, he has a lot of lessons to attend over the winter.'

The Northern Irishman is slowly developing his personality in the area, getting noticed and getting busy. I still have a feeling deep down that if he gets this right we can have a very good season. This team will not go down, but do we really do mid-table things at Swansea? When was the last time we had a mediocre, petering-out type of season? It's been a long, long time I can tell you. Maybe this time around this would do for us after two seasons of nearly and maybe. Two managers already gone in Martinez and Sousa could mean that Rodgers wants as much as us to have a mediocre time and then build on it next season. I'm not sure that the Swansea support would be happy with that, but set against the possibility of relegation, I would.

The usual rubbish surfaces in the press. Swansea are a one-man team and Scott's absence is highlighted. Once again it is the negatives which surface and these are quickly addressed by Garry Monk, a sensible chap to punch the press right on the nose. Granted, as Colin Pascoe stated after the Derby game, we didn't create enough chances – that may go some way to admitting Scott's value to the team is very real. However, we don't need to keep answering back when the press have a go. Maybe the 'group personality' that Brendan talks about will develop into a real animal with real claws. I should give Joe Allen some space here, too. He is just back in the side and is a real talent who on his day is the best midfielder in the league. He is a natural product of the youth team, and a local lad as well – from my original neck of the woods in Narberth. So even if he did look jaded, he needs game time, and we all know with that he will flourish.

It looks like Kemy Agustien will sign this week and the break from club football gives players time to reflect. Angel Rangel is willing to speak in the press about repaying the faith the fans and club have in him after injury, but his words are as cold as the October rain. I hope so, as he is always getting linked with not wanting to be at the club. If players like him and close to him really focussed and really worked hard I believe they could realise their dreams at Swansea, not elsewhere. I am reliably told that Brendan has canvassed the board as to what funds are available. Kemy was linked to us before his arrival, so I assume that after he was seen in the pre-season in Holland that Brendan liked him. I am not saying for one minute that he is a club signing. I wouldn't have thought that Brendan would tolerate that. He is still to establish himself with the board and the working relationship is developing. However, the inactivity of last season and Paulo's clear inability to not only coax players to Swansea nor offer any options may well have rubbed off on the board. I have already mentioned that agents' fees paid last season were high, and for me this indicated a club turning to agents to source players, and not a scouting or managerial ability to do so.

If the Swans board are happy to do this then Brendan needs to challenge it quickly. Managers manage and boards guide, that's the theory. Yes, the player intake is authorised at board level, but not the recruitment. That is down to a young, bright manager and his committed team of coaches.

After a boring and insignificant international break we return to action. Press action . . . then eventually football action.

Maybe Rangel's comments and compassion of late is because his girlfriend has given birth to a baby in Swansea. The lad's name is Angel Rangel. In English he will also be known as little angel. Now that could cause some confusion. Then he tells us that the new arrival is eighth in the line of Rangels called Angel. He gets the middle name of Noah, though. Congratulations Angel, you will have to watch the pennies now mate, direct debits all sorted? There are bills to pay and an extra mouth to feed. Rangel talks of spending his life in the UK and he seems happy and more settled. Maybe now with a tight family bond going on at home he will focus and see the big contract he is on as a huge bonus to playing football, and not a lever to get away from Swansea every three months. Good families ooze happiness and confidence, if this helps Angel Rangel focus away from the world of more money, agents and disorientation, it can only be good for him. It will make Swansea City the main focus as much for him as it is for me.

Van der Gun's appearance against Derby seems to have told him something as well. He is now talking about moving on from the club. He has been given some opportunities to shine, and it is clearly down to his own consistent ability as to why this hasn't worked for him. If he feels he needs to go, then I recommend he does so. I don't want to read about him leaving, this is unsettling for other players. If Cedric feels he is going to get more game time elsewhere, then he should go and do it. The unsettling nature of the Welsh press especially is once again meddling and playing with Swansea hearts. The biggest problem for me will be getting a club that will pay what he is on now. That's Orlandi's problem as well. I don't think he will find one, and the agents I speak to about this agree. He should focus and concentrate on Swansea City, not bleat on about not being here.

These players don't half get on my nerves at times. How lucky are they? Well, from my position, at times, they really don't see it. Loan them both to Wrexham – it helped Joe

Allen improve vastly and look at they type of player he is today. He didn't have that dodgy attitude though, maybe that can't be coached out of anyone?

Next up after winning at Watford is Reading, a club where the players are all saying, 'Brendan should not have been sacked'. I am told that players say this just in case the ex-manager gets a good job and comes in for them to get them a more secure, higher-paid contract. Surely footballers are not that calculating are they? Jobi McAnuff talks about this – he is a good player and for all his rotten past at another club I would say he could do a job at Swansea. Is this how I evaluate potential future signings? Look for players who praise Brendan then assume they will sign? Probably not the best method of deduction. I think I will stick with my network in the game, and maybe my own gut feeling as this season rocks on.

The game at Reading will be another huge test for us all but there will be 3,000-plus Jacks at the game, screaming the side on. The proud and loud Swansea support have travelled well this season, as they have for many seasons since it was clear we had a future.

This is great to see, although in recent years we haven't really had a bad season. And since moving to the Liberty we haven't had one at all that would be considered poor. I often wonder how our supporters would react if we were to be fighting relegation. I have already said that scenario holds no fear for me this season, and with a win today we could go fourth. The atmosphere and the day are great with Swansea supporters littered all over the place; there are no repeats of that horrible day in 1992 when Swansea supporters rioted all day along. Reading fans haven't forgotten that though, and a few comments are made in our direction. This of course sparks comments back and a few interventions are made by police and stewards – nothing to write home about though. I will say this: stewards have no redeeming qualities at all in general, if I was to stereotype. Of course like in all occupations you do meet the odd one or two who restore your faith. I think they really do need to realise that when you lay hands on a person you are entering the realms of assault and legality that could cause them real problems. And of course defences of self-defence. It's proper training they need, not the desire to see a free game of football at their home town club.

The game itself sees the return of Scott Sinclair and we are revitalised for the ninety minutes. Masses of vocal support cheer on the Swans and Scotty supplies us with a 1–0 half-time lead. Radio Wales report a thousand Jacks at the game, but one-sided bias seeps through again as the attendance is announced at over 3,000. Poor reporting is best kept in the dark corridors of North Korea, not North Canton. The Swans were quick and slick with Sinclair and Dyer probing and cajoling the Berkshire team's defence, hitting the bar and Dobbie tormenting them throughout the game. David Cotterill is getting more game time and his thread-like passes are an asset when the game breaks down in midfield. Shane Long is a threat though, and he looks a cut above the rest Reading have on offer. He just needs to wind his neck in and close his mouth for five minutes, it may be the making of him. It's hard to find anything passionate to say about Reading's makeshift support. They have Henley-on-Thames and Goring on their doorsteps – genteel places of Englishness that hardly spawn zealots. And that is very clear. They need steel, pride and passion as my mate Howard would say.

Reading could have got back into the game, but they didn't. They could have scored, but they didn't. Swansea could have scored a few more, but they didn't. No bookings and no red cards again doesn't take away from the commitment, but the Madjeski Stadium needs waking up – they are the poorest fans I have seen yet this season (and I have been to Watford). They need to forget their prejudice and channel their voices pitchside to their team, not rely on twenty under-14s to wave sheep across a guarded divide. What a sterile atmosphere, the only noise coming from a solid and loud Swans support. The team should be proud. And yes, tonight we are fourth in the table, well above relegation. Well on track but there are only eleven

games down. QPR head up the league with Cardiff and
Norwich above us. It is shaping up, but QPR are looking
unstoppable.

Scott Sinclair's relationship with Helen Flanagan (Rosie
Webster from *Coronation Street*) continues to blossom.
I think like all young men he needs something outside of
this glorious game. She met Scott at Wigan when he was
on loan from Chelsea. Like certain footballers today who
tweet their thoughts in a disgraceful grammatical way, Scott
needs another avenue for his life to take when the whistle
sounds and the football stops. Being with Helen Flanagan
may well cause him to become a celebrity, but I suppose
that comes with the territory as the Swans fly higher.

It sets you wondering, though, that if Scott Sinclair was
working at DVLA, would our Helen be that interested?

QPR with Neil Warnock and all roll in to town. They are
rocking along the league and bopping out opponents at an
alarming rate. If they keep this going they will be up by
February! Warnock has assembled a very decent team and
Adel Taarabt, his Moroccan magician, is firing them in from
everywhere. He is effectively QPR's Scott Sinclair. He too
gets all the press about moving, being transferred and all
that jazz, just like a number of Swansea's players. It seems
QPR are not fashionable enough for the London press, but
of course Neil knows his players and has managed them all
very well. When the going gets good Neil Warnock must
be the best manager to have in the world by your side. As I
said before, I like him, he is a real football character.

The game itself was a good one with David Cotterill
missing a penalty and all of a sudden looking deflated
and lacking confidence. If that had gone in, the result
would have been ours. Swansea controlled chunks of the
game and even though QPR had chances through Derry
and Mackie it was a fairly shared point. It does mean we
fall to sixth as Burnley beat Barnsley comprehensively.
Cardiff win as well and Watford really do put our win

against them into perspective as they beat Ipswich to go third. We are becoming used to seeing Swansea City in the top six, and that's where we are as the Carling Cup game with Wigan looms. David Cotterill is looking jaded and sadly Mark Gower is now out for a month. But what really annoys, what really gets on my nerves is Andrea Orlandi blurting his bile in the press, 'I could be playing for Leicester now' he says, just as we play them at home in the league. This football club is unique, footballers seem to lack understanding and clarity at times regarding why there are at a club. It isn't to berate fans or tell tales to the press about where they could be now. I am furious Andrea – you're ill-advised and your mindset is ill thought-out. What rationale are you working to? If it isn't the Swansea rationale, if you don't like it at Swansea then maybe it's time to move on, and do it quietly.

Sven is the manager at Leicester City. The Margaret Thatcher lookalike appears in the Championship desperately looking to reiterate his managerial capabilities. Another victim of the celebrity pack with Ulrika-ka-ka, he definitely had a rocky road at Notts County. For me, he doesn't look like the type of man that will do much at Leicester. He may threaten to, and he may convince the fans that he can. But he hasn't achieved a lot in English club football, just like he didn't achieve that much in international football. Being an ex-England manager counts for nothing, they win nothing – they expect to but never do. Wales on the other hand expect nothing, and that's what we get.

The good news is that Marvin Emnes has joined on a month's loan from Middlesbrough and he looks a diamond. He is busy and suits the Swansea style. He is a great spot by the Swansea coaching staff and he may well make a dent as we look to push on towards solidifying a top-six spot. That's not bad seeing as I would have settled with a fourth-bottom finish. Leicester will be tough to beat. Sven is new to the club and the players have a new man to impress. Maybe Orlandi can do the same? Brendan was once a Leicester target in 2007 but he turned it down, and in hindsight that was a great choice – he makes a lot of sound choices does Brendan Rodgers. He has a mentor in José Mourinho, once his boss at Chelsea where Brendan was a coach. He has a great way of deselecting options and making the right choice and this could prove invaluable as the season moves along.

What is in our favour today is that I genuinely believe that Sven-Göran Eriksson (who, incidentally, I once won £400 on when he was appointed England manager, only because I had a Sony Ericsson phone – I saw it as a an omen) does not have a clue about Swansea City. He will not know anything about us for real, his knowledge like the majority's will be totally lacking. And this turns out to be fact as we win again at home, convincingly in my opinion, 2–0. The game itself was good to watch if not a tough and hard-earned result. The crowd is 14,500 and this should cause a bit of concern as well. It really should be up around the 17,000 mark because we are now in third spot. It is nowhere near as bad as Cardiff's attendances at the same stage of their Championship journey. We are not getting 8,500 at home and average gates of 11,000 and things like that but it is a bit of a kick in the face for the board. Marvin scored the first and made the second and a 2–0 win gets us all buzzing as the talk turns to automatic promotion. I don't think so, but it's very nice to hear. On the Monday Cardiff destroy Leeds United 4–0 at Elland Road – it is an absolutely brilliant performance and this type of behaviour gets me worried as they are looking very good for promotion. The vitriolic shouts from the capital will only be that though, their long history of exploding will, I have no doubt, have us all laughing very soon.

All the posturing can now start between Wigan and Swansea. 5,200 Swans fans are journeying to the game from the four corners as Huw Jenkins calms matters down by stating that Roberto deserves our respect. It is not going to happen Huw, he is going to get his ears burned. I personally don't feel any animosity. My position is clear: the players and manager are on loan to us. The shirt and the club counts, I hold no truck with this type of hatred. He went because he wanted to, if he wanted to stay he would have. Keep it simple. If a player or manager wants to go, then let them go. If they can't offer us their heart and soul, then off they go. While with us they are very well-rewarded and extremely well-looked-after. Better than you or I could ever imagine.

The Lancashire skies are red raw with passion and the bars and pubs are brimfull of Jacks. A huge midweek support, not just because it's Roberto's team, but because the Carling Cup is getting interesting. We are a couple of games from a Wembley final. The Swans side is depleted and players who would not usually play are seen on the Wigan turf. Dorus gets a rest for Ma-Kalambay, who doesn't look as assured as our Dutchman. Van der Gun is in, Monk is left out and Kemy's playing. We didn't get the rub of the green in this game and the referee seemed very keen to go with the home team. His name is Friend, but he wasn't ours tonight. Boselli scored and Wigan went on to a deserved 2–0 victory. Martinez got the message as well – it wasn't embarrassing though, it was very well put, continuously throughout the game!

National news sites and programmes report a hot support on a chilly night in Wigan, and this is the real reason why I write this book.

Chapter Seven

Bragging Rights – Again

I f we are serious and our away form is to be taken seriously then a visit to lowly Crystal Palace should reap rewards. I am getting more and more confident as we jet along now. Scott Donnelly is in the side today, well, on the bench. He looked okay pre-season. Will we see him? Fair play to Sven, he says we are the best in the league, but that doesn't hold too much water for me, as we are the only team he has seen this season in the Championship as a manager. But it's a nice comment and makes the football world sit up for half a minute. South London and Palace is always a longer journey to get there from Paddington than it is to get to Paddington. It's most infuriating. The masses assembled in the away end are in good voice again, and the sun shines down on our white-clad men, including my old mate Orlandi who is starting to enjoy games and gain confidence. Maybe he has sneaked a quick read of the book, eh? Edgar Davids plays today for the Eagles. He is rubbish now though and certainly not the player he was. Palace, I have to say, are not good at all, and are no match for our quick passing game. There are some really clever passing moves going on – Arsenalesque at times – and we strike three times throughout a one-sided and pretty entertaining game, a point even agreed by a few Palace fans after it all finished. They loved what we did on the pitch, just wished it wasn't them or their team on the other end of it. Swansea are back to full(ish) strength with Dyer, Sinclair and Emnes tearing strips off the Palace defence and finely backed up by Rangel and a classy Neil Taylor. The performance signalled real intent. Donnelly got ten minutes at the end as well, and he didn't look out of place. If Stephen Dobbie can find some form, we will be hard to shove out of the top six.

Dorus is next to leave, this time Feyenoord want him. It's incredible really, why would he want to go there? It's approaching the toughest time of the season so far. Get through this and maybe even the most negative of Jacks will see a glimmer of hope as we go in search of the golden fleece. No backing out now Dorus. Darren Pratley's booking means he will miss the first derby clash of the season. Cardiff away: police escorts and helicopters, and a press frenzy looking for a clash of the hooligan titans. It won't happen – these games are so well marshalled that the fans can't even smell each other, let alone touch. Cardiff's danger man Jay Bothroyd will also miss the game, I don't know, maybe the FAW should have found a way of getting him a game?

George Burley joins the long line of managers rating Swansea so highly that he believes we will cruise to promotion to the Premier League. Am I dreaming?

It's Darren Pratley's turn, he is off to Newcastle this week, nice one.

What I love about the media is the way they try to predict the future. David Giles, one-time Swansea legend, predicts an easy Cardiff win in the derby game. Warren Feeney, who has played for both clubs, predicts a 3–1 Cardiff win and Uncle Tom Cobley couldn't give a toss. November is upon us and all focus is on this game. It is the mother of all derby fixtures. It has a scary history of utter madness from both sets of fans. Workplaces are divided across South Wales, and they get blurred as well because of Swansea's fine support from East Wales. I have seen police officers on duty verbal each other before these games and when the two cities' personnel police matches. I know the hatred is intense, I feel it too – intently. Dave Jones doesn't get much of a rating from his own club's fans as he always tries to play down the derby game, but in a way that comes over as if he doesn't care. Now we know he does, and it may well be that he hasn't experienced that many derby wins (Swansea hold the high ground very easily in the last fifteen

meetings). So when Dave speaks it is with good reason –
football fans, though, want passion and want to hear their
club's leader get it over in a formidable way. Unfortunately
this isn't Dave Jones' strength.

If Cardiff City win this game they will be nine points
ahead of us and the berating will begin. If they don't, the
Swans will only be three points behind them in the league
and in third place still. It is that important, nine points is
pretty decisive, three is not, and the bragging rights once
again will be ours.

The tickets are sold out, the buses are full and the escort
begins. If you are an away fan at these fixtures it all goes
'bubble' (this is the term used for a police-run trip for
visiting fans, thus ensuring no illegal combat takes place).
You have to travel from Swansea to Cardiff in an escort
and then back again. No deviations – that's the score. We
used to get an agreement for our supporters' club to join
the throng of buses at Cardiff West. Nowadays it's all too
hard, and the Valley Rams, some small supporters' club
with affiliation to Cardiff, have complained in the past of
this right of way we have. They have more issues with their
membership than we ever did at games, so we are politely
told we would have to join the mêlée at the Liberty. This
trip will take all day.

Gloucester to Swansea for 10.00 a.m., then off to Cardiff.
After the game it's back to Swansea then back to Gloucester.
The whole thought of it makes me feel sick. It will take
thirteen hours. I never enjoy these kinds of games, and I
am sure the Cardiff faithful don't either. I have enjoyed the
many victories of recent times, and the oneupmanship that
comes with it; they really do hate it when this happens, and
it happens frequently. The thing is, neither club has ever
done the double on the other in the whole history of the
league derby game – how strange.

The hatred is intense, the fires are burning and the chip
on Cardiff's shoulders is even more evident at these fixtures.
They do see themselves as Wales's premier club side – we
don't of course. The results of recent times dictate that,
but this season with both sides going well, the end league

position will determine the best club side. Both sides agree this, because both believe it will be them. The game is tight with chances for both sides. Swansea control possession and this results in persistent fouling from Chopra on Allen and Emnes. As is the case at these fixtures, the away fans are continually noisy – the allocation of 1,800 Swansea City fans just do not keep quiet – and it seems to inspire Emnes and Sinclair as they tear into the Bluebirds. Bellamy has a chance and misses, as does Sinclair who hits the post. Allen and Dyer are in with chances as well, and we dominate them. At half time it is 0–0 but I truly feel we have had the lion's share of the game, and should be winning. The looks on those Cardiff faces tells me I am not far wrong. The second half was a bit more even, but of course not that even because Marvin Emnes popped up and drove in a sweet shot to put us 1–0 up. The deafening celebrations prompted the usual Cardiff push-me, pull-me show in the crowd, but it was all to no avail, that goal would prove to be the winner. Oh joy of joys. The bragging rights once again are Swansea City's. The comments from the so-called experts are rammed down their throats as the capital city lose again, and they lose again to Swansea City, the pure white geniuses from 48 miles west. The league table never lies Dave Jones tells us, and as predicted we are three points behind Cardiff in third spot. QPR still head the way beating Reading 3–1. They are four points ahead of us, but our run of wins is proving to all that we are in the right part of the Championship, in fact in the automatic promotion spots. Maybe both Welsh clubs could go up? Cracking block Tatey – cracking decision ref.

The real cracker after predicting a Cardiff win is David Giles and only David Giles. After the Swans won, he quickly said 'I was wrong about the derby result.' No shit Sherlock! Those winter nights must fly by, mate.

From one derby game to another and it's a home defeat that hits us hard as Bristol City tame us and bring us straight back down to earth on the following Tuesday night. They looked really up for it and their flying winger Albert Adomah ripped Alan Tate to pieces. In fact he ripped everyone to pieces. This signalled to us that this league was wide open and ready for anyone who really wanted it. A Jon Stead goal very early on took away our undefeated home record – not bad to hold it until November – but the manner of the defeat was annoying after the delirium of the weekend's derby game. It must take it out of the players, all the hype and talk, but Brendan now needs to watch this carefully. We have got ourselves into a commanding position, he would be gutted if it fell away from here.

Derby are in the mix now, breathing down our necks and Cardiff, QPR and Norwich all draw, we stay third. It ain't all bad.

We can redeem ourselves this week as we play Middlesbrough at home. Marvin's loan has finished and he has shown what a very good player he is. His four-week period with us has seen him score some crucial goals and contribute immensely to the Swansea cause. The fact that he smacked Cardiff City in the mouth means he will live long in the memory. It feels like he has been with us all season and he will be a great loss.

Hull City beat Preston on Friday, and we play on the Sunday against Boro'. It will be a tough one, but we need to get back on track quickly. Cardiff's 4–2 win at Scunthorpe (they are looking doomed already) and QPR's draw at Forest means the Bluebirds are top, so we need to keep the pressure on. In among it all Scott Sinclair gets the Stuart Pearce nod for England. He is delighted that he is being recognised as an international in the Championship and then we read that Joe Allen is off to West Ham, which I find highly amusing. I bet his father (a dentist) nearly slipped and caused an orthodontic misdemeanour when he heard that. Congratulations go to Scotty though. Darren Pratley opted out of contract talks this week so I assume he is running down his contract and keeping his options open. I am reliably informed that Bolton like him ever such a lot. Are they really that appealing?

The Sunday roast is on hold as the Liberty experiences a game against once-famed Premier League boys Middlesbrough. They're a phenomena really, Boro'. They seem to have the right players, and at the start of the season the right manager. Strachan is gone, so Tony Mowbray steps in. He isn't the most enthusiastic of people but they seemed to like him at West Brom. He is a steadying influence, and maybe that's what they need.

Mowbray will come to spoil us. His tactics will not be revolutionary. Emnes won't be playing – he goes back on Monday, so he will sit this one out. I wonder how he feels? He has done himself the world of good and has been a real fillip to us over the past month. Obviously everyone wants him back, but the loan was always going to be just that – a loan – to get him games and confidence. The next time we see him he will be in a red shirt at their place. Always a tough fixture up there.

For me the side is looking more settled today . . . that is until Monk gets a knock, and Beattie, who was pretty ineffective, was substituted for Dobbie. Beattie's first-half run was pretty stunning though, I reckon he will be injured after that effort. I hope not, I do like his bustling style, I just wish it was more evident. Once again it's the media's one-man team who scores his twelfth goal of the season and in sixteen games too. Boro' did make a game of it, but we really needed this 1–0 victory in front of 15,000 Swansea faithful. It came late but when it did Scotty once again signalled to the rest of the league that he and Danny Graham are literally on fire. Tatey pickled up a yellow and by my reckoning that's him out, along with Garry Monk, for the next game. Time to test the squad again.

Sean O'Driscoll is next on the compliments board in Brendan's office. Sean plays a similar style to Swansea at Doncaster with limited players. He was a Swans target in the summer before Brendan got the job. This fixture is one I cannot make for family reasons but Rangel's equaliser late on was more than we deserved according to some; however, O'Driscoll, magnanimous to the end, does not begrudge us the point on a cold and dark November weekend. It's getting on to the end of the month and we are still third on thirty-three points after eighteen games. People are talking the talk in Swansea, and Brendan asks the question: does this team deserve a full house watching them play? Can you do that people of Swansea? My personal view is that many would if they could, but finances, Christmas on the horizon, rising and mass unemployment won't make this happen week-in, week-out as he would like. The thousands and thousands of pounds enjoyed by Brendan and the players is not the norm in these parts. The industry that once drove the city has gone in most places, and leisure and development are the new Swansea industry. The games are not overpriced and a sensible board and a sensible policy ensures this. But people will pick and choose, it's a fact of a football supporter's life. A brave signing is then made at the Liberty.

Jermaine Easter, the Cardiff-born player who has taunted Swansea fans in the past, arrives on a loan from MK Dons willing people to support him while he plays in the white shirt. If he does half of what Emnes has he will be carried off the pitch head high. A lot of Swans fans find it hard to accept Jermaine though, and won't give him a chance. That's the way it is. He has not covered himself in glory on the occasions we have played the sides he has been in, so we will have to wait and see how he fares. It's a 50/50 for me. Rodgers will also be keeping his eyes peeled for more strikers, which indicates that Beattie is still not fulfuilling the Ulsterman's requirements.

It's snowing a bit, it's cold, very cold. I have a voice deep down in my soul that is screaming, 'stay at home tonight mate, Portsmouth will come again.'

The weather was okay(ish) when we left Gloucester at four o'clock (a Friday night game) but quickly deteriorated as we progressed westwards towards the Severn Bridge. Then it got bad and my word did it snow. I wasn't too concerned as the four-wheel-drive coped admirably. Then it snowed more, and more and more and as we drove through the tolls the traffic stopped. It was quarter to five. My good mate Ian Williams was down over the Heads of the Valleys updating us on the M4, which was chock-full of cars. The journey then became worse, junction-hopping and skidding all round South Wales looking for a new outlet, for a piece of hope in a wasteland of white. There were crashes and multiple accidents. It was hell.

At Newport I conferred with Howard of Cowbridge by phone, who was in a slow-moving pile of slush, as was Ian. I turned to Andy 'What do we do?' I said. 'I reckon we should go for it, mate,' he said. I won't listen next time, Andy. The next three hours involved us using a full tank of petrol as we slowly moved towards Swansea. At twenty to eight we arrived at the game. I parked in a decent spot (I thought) then fell over on the sheet ice (three times) and at the bottom of hill by the Coopers I was overtaken by a bloke skidding on his backside towards the roundabout. 'Bloody fuckers!' he was shouting. He had fallen and taken the only course of action available to him: he adopted the 'fuck it, I'm on my arse' position and couldn't stop. As he rolled onto his side before meeting his fate on the roundabout he looked at me and said, 'Fucking Swansea City.' I knew exactly how he felt. The I fell over again, twisting my ankle. My feet and legs were frozen.

I got into the game just as Beattie scored, Andy missed it and for the rest of the game we were quite simply awful. Portsmouth did not look like a team in bother: they were slick and quick as they muscled us off the ball and ripped into us time and time again. Where did that all come from? Nugent, Kitson and Utaka did not look like League One fodder to me. They surprised me and once again signalled that there was absolutely nothing in it in the Championship. Serran had a poor game and was replaced by Agustien and Dobbie came on as well. However, it was Halford's goal in the second half after Nugent had equalised that won the game. It was well deserved, take nothing away from them. They not only bullied us right through the game, they took us to task all over the field. It was the best performance by an away side I had seen all season. I left the game only going over one more time before I got back to the top of the hill to my car and found attached a parking ticket for obstruction. This was the final insult. The weather had got worse, and at two in the morning I finally got to bed. Supporting this club sometimes pushes me to the limit. I woke the next day, still cold, but partially thawed and had to smile. The punters leaving the Liberty last night were being floored like figures in a computer game. The ice was awful. At least I suppose the game wasn't called off. It's one more in the bag for us and we are still in third. QPR later beat Cardiff 2–1, Derby lost and Norwich beat Ipswich 4–1. It is fast approaching December, and for Christmas all I want is a top six position. It's not too much to ask after my recent exploits.

Chapter Eight

Oi Mush, it's Christmas

Well, well, well Swansea City are linked with a player and it's Kevin Phillips, a player many admire as someone who will always score goals. His late arrival into football means his age is a bit of a anomaly. He could easily play up to the age of forty. Radio Wales scream 'Cardiff City's promotion push' and talk of their next game against Preston (even though they lost miserably to QPR). Jermaine Easter immediately sets about earning Swansea points in the press by stating he supports Arsenal – not Cardiff. Interesting, he has now alienated himself again. But it's only talk, he is brave enough to come to the Liberty and ply his trade. If it works he will be accepted . . . it may take longer but it will happen.

Roy Keane's Ipswich are next, an away lunchtime fixture live on Sky. Three hundred hardy Jacks are there to witness Craig Beattie play his best game of the season as Stephen Dobbie watched from the bench. Although Ipswich took the lead and dominated the first twenty-five minutes, I felt we had the edge when in possession and could have been far, far away by the time they went ahead. Andros Townsend scored the opener but really I have to say it wasn't that deserved, and for all Ipswich Town's huff and puff they looked a frightened side, a side scared to commit and reveal their true worth. Was it fear emanating from the bench? Were they so afraid of invoking the wrath of Keane that they couldn't do what came naturally?

The second half was the catalyst for the Swans' win. Just as he was about to be substituted, Beattie headed home a disputed free kick and the Swans were level. The attacks were coming from Swansea and a pathetic attempt at a clearance fell to Joe Allen who stabbed home goal number two. Ipswich continued to rally, and were shouting loudly for a penalty as Beattie's chipped shot flew into the back of the net as the game ended. The Tractor Boys were furious, the fans were furious, Roy was furious and Swansea were winning 3–1. It was a lead we were not going to let go. At the end of the game Beattie and Co. celebrated like they had won the league. They had won yet again away from home and after so many unlucky moments on their travels, it was all coming together. Brendan blossomed with pride and the players got the accolades they deserved. It was a smash-and-grab victory, just the type of Championship game that at the end of the season you look positively on. I remain hopeful that at the end of this season I can confirm that this was the game that displayed true Swansea grit.

Big John Hartson, a real fighter and Swansea man commends Beattie's incredible game, and we all hope he can produce more of the same. Both Craig and John were at Celtic and Beattie states he owes much to the big man during his education and start in the game. Big words and back-patting all round, gents. Much deserved. There is a feelgood factor in West Wales. Cardiff drew at home as their promotion push, which was much talked-about last week failed again, but they remain in second place. QPR sneaked a 1–0 against Reading as fans start to talk about misdealings in the transfer market and a potential fine or points deduction. With Norwich losing, it's Leeds who once again sneak into the top six, beating Coventry 1–0. Millwall, our next league opponents, are seventh and looking strong with Kenny Jackett at the helm. He is impressing many in South London. The press acknowledge him too, but not Swansea – we gently irritate ourselves in to third spot.

It's my birthday and we are home to Millwall on a Friday night, a game that, if won, will see us rise to second in the league. Surely then people will sit up and radio stations will talk of 'Swansea City's promotion push'? I doubt it, that is just wishful thinking, and as a Swansea fan I am the king of wishful thinking most days. Millwall home fixtures, and indeed away in recent times, have included many punch-ups between the fans and the police had to contain 2,000 Swansea fans a few seasons back in a riot outside the ground. At times that aggression is misguided and overspills into the streets around the stadium. This fixture is on a Friday for a number of reasons, but for me this is the main one. Last time Millwall came there were more ADO Den Haag supporters there than Millwall, such is the intensity of this fixture. Tonight is a bitterly cold night and the game ends all square as both sides seemed content to share the spoils. The Swans looked jaded and tired. Rangel scored from an Orlandi corner – many supporters like Andrea and when he does perform, he adds another dimension to the team. But he, too, looked tired at times and lethargic. I think Brendan will have to double his points and dip again into the transfer market in January to continue the hope we have now. Mkandawire equalised shortly afterwards, it was no surprise again, and the away form is now not being complimented by the home form. We are not losing but this could have been three points. However, a view is expressed on the way back that we could have easily lost it too – Morison, a Stevenage player just two years ago, should have wrapped up the points for Millwall. Another point gained methinks. The weekend proves this to be an accurate statement as Cardiff lose at Middlesbrough and Watford destroy QPR 3–1 away. A terrific result for the top teams – it shows they are not indestructible, they can be smashed. Leeds winning at Burnley burns through the press pages – they dearly want Leeds back in the Premier League. Their fanbase is so huge it means they must get there after so long away. A fanbase does not guarantee this – sure, it may aid finances, but look at Manchester City, twelve years ago they were in League One. I don't like Leeds.

Confirming what many thought is the press call for Leon Britton. He lays the blame squarely on the shoulders of Paulo Sousa as being the reason for him leaving Swansea. He stalks of strange relationships and no communication;

this does not surprise me, it was what I had heard from certain other players as well. I am pleased that Leon has been brave enough to speak out. I am also hearing he is very unhappy at Sheffield United. I wonder? Would we have him back? Would he want to come back? I know the answer is yes, but it would take some financial playmaking from Huw to get him in. And Britton would need to be a bit more flexible too.

We have drawn Colchester in the FA Cup but forgive me for not getting overexcited about this one. I see this as a fixture that will get in the way of our promotion push. I suppose it will give the reserve players a run-out, but my mind is so focussed on the league that it will take a huge news story or fixture to divert me. Marvin Emnes won't be coming back this season and, as he is playing out of his skin for his parent club, I didn't expect him to. I do hear, though, that he would be interested to come next season if all could be agreed, which is satisfying. Emnes really did fit in well with the style of play encouraged by a confident Brendan Rodgers. It would have been a really positive step to have got him. I am now firmly fixed on promotion. Amazing isn't it? From survival to promotion ambitions in four months – Brendan has done really well. Saturday's game against Sheffield United will be an interesting contest, we never fare well there in the league. Yes, we did knock them out of the FA Cup there 3–0 a few seasons ago, but they are a bogey club for us.

Sheffield United is yet another club that we meet with the manager gone: sacked and banished. John Carver is in charge, a man I know little about but who will no doubt galvanise his side for this game. The chef is back, Shefki Kuqi that is, his Derby loan having gone well, and I think he hopes for a return there in January. I am hearing that Nigel Clough doesn't fancy it at all, and his agent is touting him all over the place, even to four Premier League clubs, now forgive me, he isn't good enough to make that step up. He needs to be loved, that's for sure, but his age and pace surely means he won't get into the Premier League, surely that would be a daft move for any sane manager?

He does show incredible desire at times, and ten years ago was a very, very sharp and incisive striker. His goal for us at Derby last season when Robbie Savage hilariously bit off more than he could chew was absolutely terrific. But like Beattie these signs are few and far between. And I am not sure that he is fitting in to the Swansea City way at all on or off the pitch. I do know this, he won't feature in the Swansea side again this season, that surely is telling him all he needs to know about his future at the Liberty. The same goes for Gorka Pintado, he is surplus to requirements and has instructed his agent to find him another club, as has Cedric van der Gun. However, Tommy Butler is back. It's not awe-inspiring is it? He is a quality League One player for me, and will find opportunities at the Liberty very rare, if at all. However, I am not happy with Orlandi's continued role in midfield: he isn't doing it for me and Craig Beattie must be aware that Dobbie wants his shirt. It's great to have competition within the squad, but are any of these players good enough to project us into the Premier League? For me, Orlandi, Beattie, Easter, Butler, van der Gun and Serran should all make plans to move on in the close season. We need to continually evolve and search for better. Brendan Rodgers is the man to do it as well.

Apparently Scott Sinclair is suffering a goal drought. Four games without a goal is apparently a problem. I suppose it may well play on his mind since he has had a tremendous start to his Swansea career.

The game at Bramall Lane ends, as predicted, with a loss. We go down 1–0 and it doesn't fill me with joyous Christmas spirit at all. It is a game we should have won, but some grounds hold a fear for us, and this is one. We just can't do it in Sheffield. The winner is gifted to Ched Evans, a player who since his move from Manchester City has been linked to us. I don't rate him, that's why he is at Sheffield United. He is one of those players who has failed to live up to expectations. I still reckon the Blades will go down. They are right in the relegation mix, and it's when we play teams like this who will disrupt, scrap and fight for everything with little ability that points can be lost – and once again this has happened. Earlier I mentioned recalling the positive games at the end of the season – the ones where you can stand back and say, 'That mattered,' well, this is one we will look at and say 'We could have won that and got all three points.' I am very disappointed, I love winning – we all do. Tonight it's still bloody cold, the garden is dark and horrible and I think I have the first grumblings of flu. Bollocks.

We have to take a breath and look at what is happening in this crazy league. QPR have lost again, though this time it's against Leeds United and Cardiff didn't play. We are fourth in the league. For me the team to watch are Reading – they are on a run and skirting the playoff picture, as are Forest, Derby and Watford. It's so tight this year. Tonight we may be fourth, but we are also five losses away from relegation.

I get a Christmas tree for the decking outside my house from a farm market in Gloucester. I feel absolute shit and look it too. My normal glamorous complexion is as jaded as our midfield was on Saturday. I drive to the farm market and realise halfway there that I am still in my slippers and shorts. I am doing things that I cannot account for. The whole day has been strange, losing things and then finding them in odd places. Watching TV and not understanding what anyone is on about. The Varukers are on my CD player and that isn't working so I switch to Discharge and that doesn't work either. The Red Hot Chili Peppers do though – fuck, I must be ill. I get a few looks in the farm market as I drag an overpriced tree to the car, ram it in the back and speed home in an almost sterile blur of shivering. I get the tree up, get the lights on and go to bed. Maybe if I get drunk tomorrow it will go away. What the hell am I doing shopping for Christmas trees in minus temperatures in my fucking shorts?

I've had to write this next piece, the festive piece, more after the event than I would have liked. I was diagnosed with swine flu and sentenced to bed. I have never felt so ill. I was absolutely gone. The sweating flurry turned to intense chest pain and shooting lights punched their way through my head. Apparently people would pay good money for that trip. Me? I am happy just plodding along in life with a few beers and a laugh. I don't deserve this at all. I never expected to spend Christmas in bed dying and moaning. The missus has it too, what a miserable sodding mess.

You can't go to football with swine flu, you know. You may die, or at least collapse and then die. I miss two games: they are against league leaders and transfer dabblers QPR, then home to Barnsley. The Loftus test will be an interesting one, at least it would be if I gave a toss about it. As Christmas comes and goes the Boxing Day game at Loftus Road is on the radio and I am flat out in a purple haze of medication and bottled water. Every single Swansea City player either felt the same or had too much turkey. We fail in the big-game festive atmosphere in West London. QPR are on song and the thousands who travelled to support the team are on song as well – but that is where it ends. Tatey gets sent off, as does Clint Hill, who decided to run half the length of the pitch to be the hard man in a skirmish of players. I don't like him at all – he is thuggish at times for a side who are evidently favourites to go up. Neil Warnock is so animated in the highlights he looks almost deranged. Someone grabs a member of the Swansea bench, pushing and pointing at the incident as if they could do anything about the behaviour of other players. Self-defence would have been my defence – but it dies down. When down to ten men we look even worse than we did before. Adel Taarabt destroys us with two goals and further goals from Helguson and Mackie (a penalty), condemn us to our biggest defeat for some time, seasons even, and we lose 4–0. Yes 'we'. It's a group defeat: fans, players, manager, coaches, staff and board. It's very disappointing. Just over 15,000 witness the demise of Swansea City in the Christmas sun in West London.

The result hits our goal difference, which will be telling I am sure. Leeds draw and are two points ahead of us and Cardiff win too. It's a miserable Christmas present from the players to us all. The run that Reading are on is now very real: they beat Bristol City 4–1. Although such defeats do tend to send us football followers into further depths of despair, I do have a theory. Here we go again. If any side can reach thirty-five points at the end of the year they are on for whatever it is they want. It is a good starting base to push on into the next phase of the season. And with the January transfer window open in a few days, clubs can gauge what they need to do, and who they need to get in.

Swansea City can rectify this disappointing game and show it to be just a blip by beating Barnsley two days later. As this unfolds I start to hear whispers of players we may well like to get in to make the promotion push more realistic. Leon Britton is definitely one we want and Brendan admires him a lot. This will prove tricky but I am hearing that Leon will pay back his signing-on fee to enable it to happen. He is obviously keen to get away from Yorkshire. There is talk of a Chelsea player, and the press straight away go for Daniel Sturridge as the player we want. I make a phone call and straight away I am told there is no way he would come to us as there are two Premier League sides wanting him. Again the name Fabio Borini surfaces, and I am told that Brendan is very keen to get his signature. He has an agent who is well known and will be happy to allow this and advise him positively, however, beware dear Brendan, this agent is talking to an Italian club as well. His contract at Chelsea is being allowed to run down, and Brendan is slowly nurturing all involved. Chelsea will be happy for him to leave, and all are allowed to chat, talk and sort it out.

I am a fool but I allow myself the pleasure of a swine flu-infected visit to the Liberty. It is meant to be – I need a fix and no matter my physical condition (fifty per cent at best), I intend to make it to the game and support the team. I feel a lot better and hope the trip will drive away this horrible virus. Oh, by the way, I am no longer contagious at this point. Howard of Cowbridge compliments my looks by saying, 'You look like you're dead.' Cheers mate, and I get the usual 'Where have you been part-timer?' from everyone else around me in the Liberty. Bloody wurzels most of them. We huff and puff again versus Barnsley but look by far the better team. As the game moves forward Howard remarks that we should be three up; I know this, everyone knows this. If we do just sneak a win it will do our confidence no end of good. Pratley, Sinclair and Allen are on the bench, which surprises most, but tells me that Brendan isn't scared to make a decision for the greater good. Dobbie is in, as is a back four of Williams, Tate, Taylor and Rangel. Monk is also on the bench. How could this side have lost so badly at QPR? Brendan's decision to deliver a different side to the Liberty crowd displays a man who knows his own mind and who knows what it takes to get that pick-up that we need. Jermaine Easter looks busy, but at times a bit slow, while Nathan Dyer is as ever – magnificent. It takes half an hour for Easter to announce his arrival and he fires us one up. Excellent build-up play between Dyer and Dobbie allow Easter the time to take his opportunity very well indeed. The crowd's cheer has an element of relief in it, and we settle down. Now all we need to do is settle in, play as we can and secure the three points. As ever, we settle too quickly, we start to defend the lead and as the second half progresses, Barnsley have chances to not only draw but win the game. We are too slow in our passing and too defensive when it is evident that a bit more pace and sharpness of mind would knock Barnsley down. Easily.

As is so often the case this season, Barnsley sense something and it's only Dorus who manages to keep us in the game. Ash is still in West London: he is not having the best of games. Fortunately for us we have Sinclair and Pratley to come on, and both feature to secure, only just, a very hard-fought win. Joe Allen replaced Easter – it looks tactical as he has not been effective since scoring. It tightens things up, we just deserve it. And it's a commendable eighth clean sheet of the season. The 15,000-strong crowd are relieved and the journey home with the Swans on forty points, level with Cardiff in second but third on goal difference, is a pleasant one. Cardiff losing 4–1 at Watford is amusing and QPR win – again. Norwich and Reading are firmly securing themselves in the play-off spots, and Forest are still on thirty points, having played three games fewer than most. They are eleventh.

It becomes apparent to statto-types and nerds alike that Swansea City have the best possession record in the league – do you get a prize for that?

I feel much better, then lose it completely and end back up in bed after trying to dismiss swine flu as a mere passing cold. This time the doctor wants to stick things up my backside. I resist his urges and promise never to ignore him again. Swansea City will kill me at this rate. And if I am this dismissive again about such a serious illness, I fear if I do survive, my missus will kill me anyway.

Happy New Year.

Chapter Nine

Swine Flu in the Last Minute

R eading are next, Brendan's employers before his rise to managerial greatness here at Swansea. Well, he is doing better than the mad-looking Brian McDermott at Reading at the moment. If you put McDermott in a white coat and let him loose in a hospital, would he pass as a doctor or a madman pretending to be one? Eidur Gudjohnsen is linked with a move south to us from Stoke, as is Tamas Priskin at Ipswich and Jason Scotland. The latter is a big no thanks. It tells me that the manager is still not happy with the forwards' strike rate at the club. All are better than Gorka in my humble opinion, who is being linked with a club in Greece and another in Cyprus. He hasn't featured this season as we continue to rely on Beattie and Sinclair and keep our fingers crossed that neither get injured. Easter apparently has a knock.

Win against Reading and we will be at our highest league position for twenty-seven years.

I mention injuries and straight away we lose Orlandi and, more importantly, Neil Taylor in a blistering game at the Liberty. Dorus again keeps us in the game as does Adam Federici for the opposition. First we are all over them, then they are all over us. That win for the Swans earlier this season was clearly a problem for them. Brendan has enjoyed a lot of success against his two former clubs this season and it is Darren Pratley who puts us one up after Rangel hit a fine strike. New Year's Day can draw a quiet crowd, but this one is rowdy and passionate. From my sick bed I hear cries of Swansea and the commentators get carried away. For the first time they state that we are looking good for promotion. The kiss of death more like. We drive forward, then Reading do the same. Both keepers are on fine form and it could be 4–4. Howard of Cowbridge calls. He says it's a nail-biter and the New Year seems to have given us new hope: this would be a tremendous result. Kebe is a real threat and Simon Church misses a sitter. It brings to an end a game that is worth so much more than three points. Tonight we are second in the table – mission accomplished because Cardiff, who are in awful form, get battered at Bristol City and QPR lose as well at Norwich. I do feel rather unwell, and very remorseful for thinking that I am Superman, but to be sitting second tonight above Cardiff tells me one thing. We are – as I have always said – the best team in Wales. By far.

Of course as soon as I give it the proverbial 'big one' we go to Leicester City – an unhappy hunting ground for us. I sense arrogance in them as well, they believe they are supreme, edging Forest for ignorance and they posture well – but they are Leicester, of course, that is all they do. Their ground is made of crisps you know, and ear wax from Gary Lineker. I also hear that Willie Thorne's betting slips form one of the footings for the away end stand.

We have a Mr Deadman in charge today and a team in blue as opponents who reek of power and, as ever when we play them, they are quick to foul, kick and dismiss our passing game. Fair play, it works. A bloke called Bruno powered a header before Scotty popped up with a screamer, and at this point I would have bought the draw. The victory was not going to be ours today, it was written that the crisp-lovers would be victorious, they always are here as we are at our place. It's like an unwritten agreement. Vassell scored the winner. As soon as we got level Leicester were looking for it as much as we were before we scored. They had more desire, and for all my chest-thumping after the Reading victory, today is stale, a pointless game and a pointless journey for thousands of Jacks.

I see that my words will eat themselves tonight, I do not have to. We have played two games in 2011 already. In both we haven't been incredibly convincing and my remaining

lurgy is making me a negative old soul. As much as I admire
the FA Cup and as much as I love the competition, they can
ram Saturday where the sun don't shine. I need a day away
from all this, maybe a day with the family enjoying what we
missed at Christmas. Yes, that would be nice – a Saturday
without football, without tension, without frustration and
without this bloody book to update, it is becoming a noose
round my bloody neck.

The conversation starts like this, 'Well it's like love,' I
start. 'You know I have to get the book done, and to do
that it's only fair that I do as many games as I can, you
understand?' My wife looks at me, she's not getting it. So
the day that we agreed would be a family day, no football,
no writing, is now completely the opposite. I think she is
angry. Having given it some thought, I felt it best to go to
the FA Cup third round after all, and it is Colchester, so
we may win heavily and I wouldn't want to miss that. A
few slammed doors and a few misplaced comments about
marriage and me being a twat are delivered, and I agree not
to go. Instead I will spend the day with my family – and the
radio, Sky Sports News, a four-pack and a few well-placed
phone calls to those who are at the game. You see, I am not
that much of a slave to the game.

I also have to digest the news that Garry Monk is out
for a long while. When he is on form we are tremendous
at the back and Brendan will be taking a risk if we don't
look to replace him. The Colchester game wasn't attended
by the madding thousands at the Liberty, and after the
game their manager, John Ward, joined the many adding
to the compliments board in Brendan's office. We did
hammer them. In the end it was 4–0, and could have been
a lot more. I did have a nice day with the family, grandson
included. He has the look of a number nine you know.
Overall, as I settle down tonight and see that once again we
have drawn the football greats of Leyton Orient in the FA
Cup, I realise what an idiot I have become. Team's fans like
Orient supported us in our hour of need, let's not get too
complacent, it won't take much to go shooting back down
there. I welcome the FA Cup draw – we will never get the

so-called greats at the Liberty in the cups, so let's just look forward to hammering them when we get promoted. Yes, I welcome Leyton Orient. They deserve to have their day, and looking at our injury list and reserves they may well do. It's live on S4C too, so look out!

Monk's injury means Tatey is the captain until Garry returns. Scans are showing that his injury could be a done deal in six weeks: I hope so, he is a loss. Mark Gower is in the press talking about getting in fresh faces, and Huw says that all new contract talks will wait until the end of the season so we know where we are. Fair enough, a bold move, and one that I respect based on the fact the board won't jeopardise the club like many do. They have the club at heart, so all those players can now be quiet, stop going on about more money and settle down and do their jobs, for which they are handsomely rewarded. Nice one Huw. Players – listen, and wear that shirt with pride.

That of course doesn't stop the talk about players leaving. Ash is still getting the Newcastle United treatment and apparently a bid is imminent. Mind you, when you see the source of the news report – Talksport – I have to smile, and then burst out laughing. They know nothing. £6 million will get his services though, that much I do know.

Lopez has been moved on and released and the great news is this allows us to bring Leon Britton back to Swansea. He has been desperate to return as we know, and this is now fact. He pays back his signing-on fee (as predicted) and joins as he left, for nothing. What a great acquisition. January is hotting up and Brendan is bullish about continuing the effort and getting more players in, great news.

Crystal Palace are despatched with ease at the Liberty as the transfer window provokes all sorts of speculation. Scott Sinclair converts two classic penalties in the 3–0 win on a quiet day at the Liberty – the fans are restless and nowhere near as noisy as usual. The call is for a drummer to be injected in to the East Stand – yes, an annoying banging to our right will be heard from now on. In fact, on reflection, I quite like the idea. It makes me feel all Continental. Darren Pratley gets a few heckles from his fan club over his persistent whining in the press and failure to agree terms. It's sure to happen as long as he continually harps on. But he scores a cracker in any event, which is apparently the best way to answer your critics. I'm not sure about this, indeed if I was to answer my critics in work by scoring goals in a net conveniently placed in the corner of our office, I probably would get the sack. An easy victory puts us into second place again, above Cardiff who drew with Norwich and hot on QPR's heels. They draw 0–0 at Burnley and Leeds win again, 4–0 against Scunthorpe who look more doomed than the last time I mentioned them. Watford won't go away either, they beat Derby 3–0 at home and are sixth. The Swans are now on forty-six points, with QPR on forty-nine. It's getting interesting.

Darren Pratley will be a West Ham player by the end of the month apparently. Kuqi will be released this week and Ferrie Bodde (the firm Swans favourite) has doubts cast on his future. This is a great shame but he has broken down after three cruciate injuries, so can we really expect to see the man again in a white shirt? Whatever happens he was a part of what got us where we are now, and everyone will remember that.

Next up are Barnsley away, another of those not so great places to go for Swansea City.

Sky TV get involved and show an interest in our game against Leeds United next month, so the game is switched to a 12.45 p.m. kick-off. I am asked in work about the possibility of Swansea getting promoted, and do I think we will be allowed to go into the English Premier League. It's a good question if you know nothing about football and Swansea's ninety-year affiliation with English football, or if you are an idiot. The person asking the question is a Liverpool supporter, oh, how grand you are young man. I could have buried him where he stood. He has never seen them play but states he will do if they play Swansea. He says he could come with me. I reply quite honestly that if that ever happens he should get his tickets from the same place he gets his season ticket to watch Liverpool. 'I haven't got one mate,' he says.

'Exactly,' I reply.

Barnsley's ground is at Oakwell, and they have had a ferocious following in recent years. Their manager is Mark Robins who used to play for Manchester United. He has done a marvellous job since arriving from Rotherham, where he also did a himself proud. He is a bright young manager for sure. Talk is also about the return of Jason Scotland, which I do not favour at all – he is too old and slow, his time has come and gone at Swansea, unlike Leon Britton who is described as a 'king' by Brendan. 'The king has come home!' he proclaimed. He then starts him on the bench at Barnsley, easing him gently, which we all agree is wise. Jazz Richards starts today as well, a rare chance for him and right at the last minute Luke Moore joins the party. Rumours abound about how much he cost – and his wages are in free flow. He hasn't had great press at West Brom who must love us when we give them a phone call. And at Villa he petered out after a promising start to his career. Loans at Wycombe and Derby weren't the greatest of times for him either, but he does have presence, and, when he wants to, a bit of pace. It doesn't sound like a desperate move for a man who is far better than Easter whose return to MK Dons was a clear signal he wasn't what we were looking for and that we would continue looking. For me Moore is a similar, but better player, than Easter. I suppose that makes him a good signing. And one who is better than what we have already in Craig Beattie, I assume. I am not so sure: I think he is the type of player who needs constant inspiration to keep going. If that is what he needs at least we have a manager who can do that in Brendan. I hope he can, he hasn't done much wrong with anything else. He is clearly enjoying working with Alan Curtis and Colin Pascoe, too. We are becoming quite a firm and professional team – it all seems to be gelling at the Liberty.

Barnsley did the same sort of thing to us at Oakwell as they did at the Liberty. They were quick and at times ruthless in the tackle, but didn't have our class and passing game. They had a goal chalked out from my old mate Danny Haynes, and went ahead through a good Hassell header. It is a hassle too, indeed they nearly scored again straight after that. We needed to steady the ship and did so quickly before scraping along to half time still 1–0 down. It was all looking a bit similar in the second half but Dobbie came on and changed matters, I knew he could you know. Just give him a shot at it. Then Britton got on and we stated to look more like the old Swansea. It all came to fruition when Scott took matters into his own hands and was brought down by the Tykes' keeper, Luke Steele. He converted the penalty, and Luke Moore failed after that to win the game. Today he could be covered in glory instead of mud. However, I am happy with 1–1. Mark Robins isn't and complains about stuff on the radio as we listen on the way home. I used to like him as well. You should be happy Mark, it could have been worse. You could be at Rotherham, who I don't like at all.

With Cardiff beating Watford 4–1 we lose second spot, but we travel another game closer to the end of the season. I reckon we can make it to the play-offs but everyone else still thinks we can win the lot. Fair play, that's better chaps. We have regained our optimism – I reckon they missed me you know. Chips on the way home, fresh beer in the fridge from my mate Stokesy and it's still Saturday when I get home. Terrific.

I then watched the Leyton Orient FA Cup game on S4C as the band jammed away for a show at the end of the month. Orient deserved to win (great goal Tatey), now we can concentrate on the league and the visit of that lot from down the road.

We manage to capture David Edgar from Burnley just at the end of the month by all accounts. I am not sure about him at all. Last season when on loan he got ripped apart at Bristol City, and I mean totally ripped apart. I reckon he must still be feeling it. No, for me, it's a wrong move.

The month of February starts with a few local derbies – the Severn derby, as it is called, is on a Tuesday night at Ashton Gate. Edgar doesn't feature tonight, and I am quite happy about that. We all meet up at Aztec just by the M5. A thronging clan of Jacks, myself included, head for the best kebab van in the West Country, if not the world. Check him out: he parks opposite the entrance to the Hilton. Bloody fantastic kebab van, fresh and clean too. Just what the hungry travelling midweek fan requires. Kev is impressed – I can see just how impressed by the state of his dribbly chin. After a good munch and Andy's world record attempt at eating too much of everything, it is a slow drive to the ground, it takes an age. The reason is a simple one, there are thousands of Jacks trying to get to the game. I blag a parking spot at a nearby business premises (it's murder parking at Ashton Gate) and we are in the ground. There's no sense of trouble – there never really has been at these games. I am told everyone knows who the real men are. The Swans have sold some 1,600 tickets for the game but Bristol City say it's alright to pay on the gate. This creates anarchy owing to the fact that far more fans than anticipated turn up. There are thousands everywhere, I am told outside. Maybe a slight exaggeration as the away end is just about full, generating a nice little bit of revenue for Bristol City as well. It's not exactly reflected in the away attendance though. Interesting.

We destroy them, we totally destroy them. From start to finish Bristol City did not have an answer to our game, it was a thing of sheer beauty, sheer class. All the hard work was paying off and the 2–0 victory does not tell the tale. Britton dominated, Pratley got the goals (he scores very important goals does Darren), Moore and Gower were constantly an outlet and the back four were rarely threatened. They were magnificent, it was total football throughout. The travelling Jacks boomed their voices through the Bristol night air and we celebrated a fantastic away win. Even afterwards the opposition fans agreed that we were unbelievably good, the best they had seen all season. All except one fat bloke who clearly had drunk too much cider over the years . . . he said, 'I reckon if we could have scored three, mate, we would have won.' Well, that was a gem mate – do you reckon? Problem is you didn't have one chance all night, let alone three. Apparently he was later spotted on the A38 directing traffic and looking for aliens. What a nutcase.

Remember that report that Darren Pratley was definitely going to West Ham by the end of the Talksport month? He did well tonight for a West Ham player, eh? Why would he want to go there? He would be playing Championship football again next season and at this rate, we won't be. What a night.

It's boiling up for derby day again as Dave Jones, the Cardiff City manager, makes his usual bizarre and nonsensical pre-derby comments about Swansea City's finances. He sounds like a lunatic at times. He even berates himself when he speaks – a terrible loser even before the game starts. It is almost as if he is laying the foundations for another Cardiff loss. Talking about our finances? We are run by the fans mate – punters who pay and support the community. Mind you, as derby games go this one will probably go the way of Cardiff or be a draw, we can't get the double over on them, can we? It has never been achieved before, so why now?

The Cardiff fans endure the usual bubble trip nonsense which we all know and are accustomed to. They arrive in their shed-like vans and the derby literally kicks off from the moment they arrive. I don't enjoy these occasions. They are fine afterwards, after a victory, but beforehand and during they are hard going. I know Cardiff fans who think the same way. There is a lot riding on these games, you see.

The top six remains tight, and our position in third behind Norwich and QPR is a precarious one. If we can get a result today then Cardiff will be beneath us, five points away. If they win they go above us, it'll be all change in the league table. The game was severe. A really hard-fought affair, and Craig Bellamy was the difference in a tough and competitive game. The Swans had enough chances to bury Cardiff throughout the match and when Bellamy scored the winner right at the end of the game, he displayed once again his immature outlook on life by goading the Swansea fans in front of the East Stand. One got on the pitch in a sincere attempt to attack him, while others did the same towards the Cardiff fans. Bellamy really should buy himself a brain. He was so carried away that he had no idea what he was creating among the less tolerant in the big crowd – it was very foolish for such a talent. It isn't a case of the fans should know better – the players have equal responsibility here. The fighting in the crowd after he started his antics was not pleasant to see, and I blame him for instigating it. Okay, the people involved thereafter should know better, but so should he. People got hurt because of his behaviour. However, I grant that the talent he is and the goal he scored was a tremendous strike, worthy of saving Cardiff City's blushes for another season. The game could have gone either way. Funny though afterwards, Dave Jones suddenly cared about the derby game again, when all the other times he has lost he hasn't. Odd that, eh? Give them their five minutes of fame, I will settle for this if we go up. It is, after all, their first ever win at the stadium.

Jason Scotland has issued a come-and-get-me plea to Swansea and I find that quite funny as his wages are incredibly high for what he does and what he can offer. Swansea City won't pay those type of wages, Jason. Halve them and maybe they will, but no way will the club that made you break themselves for your bank balance.

Paul Jewell (Roy Keane's replacement at Ipswich), is also clearly misguided and too used to what football can give him to understand at any level what we have at Swansea. When will these people who use football for high salaries and don't care what happens to the club after they go get a reality check? Honestly, what a joker. He is just disappointed we don't want Jason Scotland, who I can assure you has seen much better days.

The league table is packed tight and looking very unstable. Teams are hopping over teams every week: this week we are fifth. And I will add to that we are fifth and loving it!

I remember Gorka scoring a belter last season at Middlesbrough, and I would settle for that today as the Swansea express goes to the north-east. February is a gruelling month. Gorka has gone though, and we hit town ready for a real battle. Middlesbrough are a changed side with Tony Mowbray in charge, and they have that little diamond Emnes to worry us as well.

I was right to worry about him as well because Boro' fired themselves into what looked like an unassailable 3–1 lead, Emnes lashing in a super strike. However, Boro' and the hardy few at the game did not take into account this new Swansea spirit. The Cardiff game is behind us and we mean business. Nathan bagged a rare goal in a frenzied opening twenty minutes, but Boro' took their chances. Scott got a penalty via Joe Allen and converted it to make the score 3–2, and then later Ash somehow forced home the ball for 3–3. I had settled for a point but Craig Beattie hadn't, and his winner brought about a huge and massive celebration with Brendan on the touchline. This is the Swansea spirit we longed for, and now we are seeing it most weeks. The fight and the guile are like steel, and in a rough and tough area this is the best way to have that steel tested. What a fantastic victory for football. This is the type of game that leaves you breathless and needing a stiff drink. It tests your very soul, and drains you completely. Results elsewhere confirm the importance of this excellent win. Cardiff, Leeds and Norwich all win, QPR draw and somehow Ipswich win 6–0 at Doncaster. We are still in the top six, four points ahead of the challenging seventh-placed Leicester City. It is a very important win, make no mistake.

Brendan has revealed he bases a lot of his coaching mindset on Barcelona, having spent time there watching them and increasing his managerial competence. He is in the right position now to push forward the Swansea football philosophy. He has added goals and steel to the team that lacked so much last season. His belief in himself and his players is tangible.

As February marches on we have Doncaster next and I expect, no I demand, a win. This will give us fifty-six points and if, as I expect, Cardiff lose at a rejuvenated Forest, we go above them into third place. The team answer my call and everyone else's as we splendidly deliver a severe blow to Doncaster's league position and hammer them 3–0. I left the stadium thinking that this was in a way a bit of a loss. We could have scored any amount of goals and O'Driscoll admitted he had no answer to Swansea's total football and total dominance. Even a flat tyre on the way home did not deflate me. And I was right. Cardiff lost and we went above them. This football lark is a breeze, not at all like some would have you believe. Heartache? Nah mate, this is an absolute pleasure.

We are level with Forest who are second on fifty-six points. QPR draw at Preston who are fighting for their lives. It's definitely on, and we are looking like we want it so, so much.

Chapter Ten

You Are Who?

I've spent all week thinking the impossible since the Swans' smash-and-grab win at Coventry City. It seems as well that people are beginning to believe the impossible dream too. Over 1,200 away supporters at the Ricoh on a miserable Tuesday night in February tells one tale, the absolute delight when Stephen Dobbie scored the winner definitely tells another. Walking away from the ground and noticing the smiles and the upbeat gait of the Swansea fans fills me with a real positive glow. And Brendan Rodgers seemed to enjoy it as well, he must genuinely believe he is a part of something huge. This is the way it is at Swansea – he will know that already. For me though, his quote about his players and staff just inspires me; true or not, I don't care, but Brendan believes that his squad are not too fussed about diamonds and cars and are more focussed on real-life events. 'Living in Swansea gives you a real sense of humanity,' he says. My word, he is falling in love with the place like so many have before, I can see a glint in his eye, a shining beacon of fulfilment building. If this carries on, he will end up staying here. He may even end up fishing the Tawe!

The Coventry performance tells me as a football fan what is happening at a club just under the surface. I see it at many clubs, but rarely at mine. It feels like Blackpool's late run last season when they pipped us and everyone else who wanted to be involved to that play-off spot all had worked hard for over their forty-six games. This time in Swansea though, it's beginning to feel like a whole lot more. We have fifty-nine points chalked up already and thirteen games to go – win five or six and it's definitely the play-offs for us, win eight, potentially nine, and I reckon it'll be automatic promotion. Am I being a realist based on what I have seen, or an opportunist, unlike so many Swansea strikers of recent times? And tonight the results have really gone our way. Norwich slipped up at home to Doncaster, and Leeds United dropped points at home to Barnsley to bring a huge smile to all who hear those wonderful nuggets of good news emanating from radios all along the M42.

The big thing for me now is injuries. We have been so lucky so far this season. Many Swans fans will tell you that we have had a torrid time on the injury front over the past few seasons. The squad has lost player after player to an astounding number of cruciate ligament and back and shoulder injuries that have even led some to question the training sessions and make-up of the training week. Others look to the Liberty pitch with its small percentage of plastic twine permeating through the real stuff. However, this season we have a new manager, and a new focus that's for sure. Is it that the training has changed? Could it be that Paulo Sousa and Roberto Martinez did things so differently that players got injured in between games? It's just a question, but I think a valid one.

The build-up now is in real time and is almost tanglible. I hear of the mass Leeds United invasion of Swansea come this Saturday and I think back to the 5–1 thrashing we gave them back in 1981. Back then the Swans really did fly and broke real hearts. That day, for anyone who witnessed it among that 25,000 crowd, will be firmly etched into their memories. It wouldn't have mattered who the Swans played that day – they would have battered them, that's for sure. It was one of those points in history that meant so much. When games like this Saturday surface you always recall the time you did them properly, when you routed them so well they were out on their feet. It is, after all, Leeds United. I don't like them as a team and never have done – there is a sense of arrogance about them as fans and players that makes them unappealing and difficult to have any sympathy for. 'Dirty Leeds' most will tell you – well, I don't think they deserve any sort of comparison, good or bad. I can't stand them.

I feel a certain trepidation as this fixture looms next for us. It's a real test. Leeds have lost one out of twenty games or something frightening like that. They got massacred by Cardiff City earlier on in the season, but that was a freak game. They could perform well at home as we found out at Elland Road, although that had more to do with us playing badly. Speaking to Leeds fans who ventured to that game, they all believed the Swans to be an awful team, and very much in a false position now. They may be in for a shock if that opinion also runs through their team.

The cameras are down for this one again. The focus on Swansea City is moving on a little bit from the ignorant *Football League Show* comments about misleading league positions and playing above their game. Now the TV is wheeling out Gary Speed – why, I don't know. Every time I see him I thank our lucky stars he was never appointed as Swansea manager, what were they thinking? Big John Hartson is in the vicinity I'm told, and I wonder if he is a Liverpool fan or a Swansea fan today? I will admit I do know where his heart really lies, but he does get caught out now and again. The big man is a real battler, so I won't rib him too much here, suffice to say I could tell one or two tales about him. My good mate Phil and I, when we wrote Roger Freestone's biography, were privy to a Welsh training camp at the Vale of Glamorgan Hotel over a four-day period in 2002. As much as I thank our contact at the FA of Wales for sorting it out, I can understand why they were reluctant to give us such a high level of access to the players. They are living the dream that's for sure. I'll come clean – John the Jack has proven to be a special type of Swansea fan since his return from a potentially killer illness and I reckon he has few unfulfilled ambitions. There has to be one though, that white shirt and a goal in front of an adoring Swansea support maybe? John chose his own pathway, and when he wanted to sign for us, the club had moved on. We saw a man who dearly wanted to play for his home town club, but who had stolen that right away from himself to an extent when he signed for West Bromwich Albion. Anyway, welcome home today, John.

My travelling companions today include one Leeds
fan from Gloucester – he seems confident too. Smugly
confident? Maybe. I don't hate him of course, it's just the
football thing I've spoken of previously. Our journeys west
to Swansea are rarely filled with incident and conversations
generally centre around our expectations regarding the
result, who may well be the pivotal man of the match –
stuff like that. Today, however, there is a stream of away
buses and minibuses on the motorway. The compulsory
'V' sign and a tremendous moon from the rear of a Tetley's
coach are met with applause and laughter. No resentment
or violence is felt nor dealt with, but what is noticeable
is the springlike weather. Warm sunshine with hailstones,
followed by rain, as the 50mph limit speed traps hit us all
along the M4 from the Severn Bridge to Bridgend. Wind,
cloud, rain, 'V' sign, moon and sunshine all fill our journey.
Then, as if he was meant to be a part of our script, a frantic
head-slapping apparition appears in the fast lane, swerving
and moving into position. The way he slaps his head then
cuts across to the middle lane signals an individual either
on medication or urgently in need of some. His daughter
in the back of the car is joining in like an ape on acid,
perilously close to her own demise as her father, in charge
of the vehicle, brakes hard and disappears off at junction
28 towards High Cross. As I reflect on this brief encounter
with our head-slapping friend the lasting image is one of a
child frothing at the mouth (probably overfed on Clark's
pies) whose upbringing one could only probably describe, if
asked, as interesting.

As our latest case study angrily departs the script, our
Leeds chum is silent. Only after 5 miles does he say, 'He
wasn't happy lads, did you cut him up?' My response can
only be 'No mate, it was an unexplained moment in our
football supporting history, the fact we were both in cars is
purely coincidental.' We head on to Swansea Bay. The vista
of Port Talbot and the bay appears again when incident
number two occurs. A car towing a small trailer explodes
and blocks the motorway for 20 minutes. As we pass the
debris it's hard to imagine what has happened. Wooden

planks are strewn across the M4: clearly an explosion here lads, and a most confused-looking farmer-type scratching his head as the wind lifts off the hat of an attending constable. Here are real lives in motion, in full view and for all to see. Our collective assessment of what might have happened ranges from exploding gas bottles to exploding farmer's daughters.

These early kick-offs are getting more frequent for the club and this is the earliest of the season, a 12.45 kick-off is just a bit too early after a decent Friday night with Mr Smirnoff. I'm old enough now to know my limitations, and being the driver of our happy band, it's good to know if I were to explode it would be relatively alcohol-free. Junction 45 is next, it's packed with hot fuzz and queueing cars moving onto the final carriageway to the Liberty. Our journey ends with a decent parking shout on Cwm Level Road again, and Rossi's is our only hope of sanity. It's a great spot to watch the visiting supporters arrive in coach after coach with a traditional Swansea welcome. Hand gestures from Swansea City to you, our friends from Yorkshire (and indeed all points north, south, east and west of Leeds). Then, for me, there's a funny moment. A man, aged I would say about fifty or so, decides the burger queue is not the place for him to be. He literally sprints into position as the red lights change to green on the main road and shouts repeatedly 'Where were you in '81?' Looking at the occupants of most of the coaches I would say they were either in nappies or wondering how the leg of their Action Man could have fallen off overnight. Once he has delivered his question, he moves slowly back to the burger van, and as he does so he casts a lonely figure as he realises the queue is now fifteen deep, and how unfortunate that he was so close to that cheeseburger before his Tourettes kicked in.

So, 'Dirty Leeds' we will call them, for that, in banter terms, is what they are and always have been. I can recall well the likes of seeing Bremner, Hunter, Cherry, Clarke, Gray, Jones and Sprake (oh Gary, your careless hands in front of the Kop at Anfield will live forever) – they ruled supreme in the early to mid-1970s. This was the Dirty Leeds so intent on misconduct that they masked a great team, the side that had so much ego and violence running through them that they managed to oust the greatest manager the country has produced – Brian Clough. Hard as nails and twice as strong, their encounters with Chelsea enthralled me as a kid, and looking back now there is so much difference from then to today's game as we know it. This current Leeds team should be proud of the fact they are linked with such great names. Franny Lee once decided that he had seen enough of the Dirty Leeds tactic of unadulterated violence and took matters into his own hands. The spiralling punches he landed on Norman Hunter's hooter were so fantastic to see that I think the whole country applauded. Norman teetered on the brink of being outpunched by a far smaller man as both left the field after being sent off. What brilliant memories of a time when footballers had far more respect than they do today. Their belligerent attitudes haven't changed that much, though. However, they have far more money to count over a quiet weekend, so I am sure they don't mind that much.

We must get to the game. The entry in to the stadium was littered with hopeful Swansea supporters of all ages. It has to be said the new stadium, as it still is, has to be a better place for football to be watched by the more discerning punter. My thoughts go back to that Leeds game in 1981 – there was a real smell of hatred about that day as fans clashed all over the city. The Specials were booming out shouting 'Gangsters', and skinheads were rife, with clenched fists passing by us in huge mobs of vengeance. Northampton Lane provided the base for punks and skins to gather as Swansea's finest in groups of two, three and four hundred ran towards the Quadrant as the police tried to regain control in the bus park. You don't get that at the Liberty. But you do get a decent curry and chips.

Today's team is without Darren Pratley and Leon Britton as starters. I get the feeling Darren is being rested, or is Brendan looking deeper into the player's psyche? I do feel Darren is paving the way for his leaving of the club that made him. Is Brendan aware of this and preparing for a season after this one when Darren is likely not to be a Swans player, regardless of the outcome? Who can say, but he has been dropped to the bench a few times of late. The side looks solid, almost unassuming to the outsider, but a team is gathering here. Mark Gower is at last showing real promise alongside Joe Allen with Nathan Dyer and Scott Sinclair (he knows Rosie Webster you know) firing on all cylinders. Is there a place for Pratley today in any event? Luke Moore looks like he is seeing for himself what can be achieved at Swansea, but we need a goal from him today, and the back four looks solid under the guidance of a happy and contented Dorus de Vries. Today is a watershed and all of us know it.

The sun is shining, and some of us will walk high above the clouds on this game all week. From the start it seems we as a team and as a support have everything to prove to the visiting Sky cameras and the adoring near 20,000 crowd. The atmosphere is fantastic, and the flowing, passing style of our game is wearing Leeds down from the off. They hate it. It doesn't take long for them to start the usual hacking and fouling and complaining to ref Phil Dowd who has heard it all before from pitiful Manchester United players. We totally outplay them, scoring early on from a wonderfully worked Scott Sinclair piece of play with Luke Moore. The stadium explodes. It's deafening. The Swans pass and pass to overtures of 'the Jacks are going up!' from the converted thousands. No rugby today, as the Welsh team struggle to victory in Italy, a full ground means that the club will not be worrying about international events such as a match with a funny-shaped ball in Rome. Wales is a country with an apparent real passion for rugby. That may well be so, but more people watch football and play football in Wales than rugby. You work it out. Leeds manager Grayson seems consumed with anger and it starts to rub off on his players. They hack some more at Sinclair, Dyer, Allen and Gower, giving away free kick after free kick. They have so many players booked it seems inevitable they will finish short. Then Tate decides to chest away a firm cross into the penalty area, now he has done this before already this season, and it looks similar to the lawful chest-away against Cardiff in November. Replays display a different view, and it should have been a penalty, but we had no replays at this game, just a pretty poor linesman who was hopeless throughout the game. That brief Leeds response was escaped and the second half was a display of pure football for us all to enjoy. Leeds were so badly rocked by our passing game they couldn't argue when once again they brought Dyer down in the penalty area. This time the penalty was given, cue Sinclair and cue celebrations unrivalled since the win at Cardiff. Cue Leeds United completely falling apart. Enter Luke Moore, it's now 3–0 and it could have been so much more. Leeds somehow survived with eleven men on the pitch, and their complaints afterwards were evidence, if anyone needed it, of why so many fans of so many teams dislike the club and all that goes with it.

Tonight my beloved Swans are second in the Championship, regardless of what happens elsewhere in later kick-offs.

It's 11.00 p.m. and I'm in a haze of reflection after watching the game again on Sky and again on *The Football League Show*. At last a decent post-match analysis on the Swans from Leroy Rosenior – the one-time Gloucester City manager compliments the levels the side has reached today. I'm proud of our achievements, I've had so many text messages it's mad, all complimenting me on my team. Why? Do they think I have anything to do with the way we play? I must say though, if the next few Tanglefoots go down as well as the first three, I may well have to reconsider. I am starting to believe.

Football, like life, and indeed the wife, has a way of kicking you in the temple just when you think you have got to grips with the whole thing. This week is spent in a relative football heaven type state, and due to certain work projects I only have access to the internet and the chosen few I now travel with. Okay, I get the odd phone call from on high, those wonderful people who consider me a part of their daily routine, but there is little news about, and little news means the rumour mill will kick in through boredom. This is a football fact.

On the various Swansea City websites I read of promotion and Premier League football. I see little, if any, notes of caution. Okay there are a few, but the main thrust is that the Swans are going up. This third season in the Championship has seen us better equipped to do so, that's for sure – in fact looking back on the past two seasons I am very glad indeed we haven't made the leap into the Premier League, as we would probably be back in the Championship by now and maybe even staring at that League One abyss. This is the Swansea City way, the fans' way in any event. Cloud any silver lining with despondency and negativity. I am getting all the wrong vibes about this week's fixture away at Scunthorpe. I am reliably told that they employ ground staff, but that's where the similarity ends to pruning and preening the playing surface. I don't blame Scunthorpe at all, they are scrapping away at the bottom end of the table and have had a decent set of results, especially against higher-positioned teams at home. Forest are one side they despatched 1–0 at Glanford Park two weeks ago. My fears are confirmed as I get a few reports that clearly state that Glanford Park will not be the home of free-flowing football come this Saturday. In fact the quagmire that they call a pitch will do nothing to encourage a game of passing football at all. I hear Brendan is none-too-happy with this either, but football is football and I know he will approach this game in the way he approaches them all. Positively and with an eye on the victory.

I don't travel to Scunthorpe. I have three games pencilled in out of the next four for definite (which means much expense) and something had to give. The lure of North Lincolnshire is not strong enough for me to want to spend a weekend there, or a day out. I know of some who spend hours walking through dampened fens looking for a wild bird in the hope it will appear for a few moments. That for them is a decent day out, while most Swansea City fans' experiences of looking for wild birds will centre around a hunt through the various fast food outlets around the Kingsway and Wind Street on a Saturday night. The Scunthorpe ground is grey and purpose-built, and the support is generally poor, but I will give them this – they can be aggressively noisy. Put this in the mix with a poor pitch and, well, you never know. That isn't my reason for not going, that's the truth, the reason is the same reason why most won't go. It's horrible.

The after-match report talked about a dire pitch, total Swansea domination and, again, the importance of taking our chances. Yes, you guessed it, the Swans lost 1–0 to a disputed penalty, having had one ignored themselves at the other end. Just deserts I hear you Leeds fans say – what goes around comes around is definitely a phrase for this season. I've learned that much. The state of the pitch was appalling, bordering on questionable. Brendan Rodgers backs this up by stating, 'The pitch was almost unplayable at times.' The Scunthorpe manager, Ian Baraclough, clearly knows only one way to scrap his way out of their current misfortune. For me if that is all he has in his locker, he won't last long as manager at Glanford Park. There is a two-way street here, and we either are equipped enough to deal with teams like Scunthorpe or we are only able to play on certain surfaces. Either way, the top of the table is getting a tad compact, and it looks very healthy for the likes of Burnley or even Watford to come through. And then there's Hull City. We have to play all three over the next two months. All three of these teams are, for me, quite capable of making the play-offs. The Swans have Watford next, and an excellent opportunity for the team to put to bed their awful result at Scunthorpe United.

The thing is, if these terrifying three are all capable of making the play-offs – who will be making way? Cardiff City losing at home to Ipswich comforts me somewhat, but surely it won't be them?

Chapter Eleven

Twit Off, Please

The problem with Swansea City is that they don't let you rest on your laurels for long. Even in March. My moan today is that players need to move away from this cursed thing they call Twitter. Ashley Williams loves it, and many other players, current and of old, seem to as well. News today hints at players getting huge fines and bans for using this social network, and I wonder if this will actually happen and be written in to FA law?

In any event, the tiredness brought on by an ever-demanding season continues tonight at home to Watford, a team who were comprehensively beaten over eighty minutes at their place, and then with the Swans 3–0 up, came back to 3–2, and should have got a point. They have this Danny Graham character too. Huw will tell you that the club have admired him for a good two years, this much I do know, and I feel we may well be back for him come the summer. I have seen this wonder kid they call Graham on many occasions – he is quick, quicker than Tate, more skilful, far more skilful than Neil Taylor (at the moment) and has amazing anticipation. For me he is quite simply the business. And for all the talk of him joining the Swans, I will let you know now, it was never going to happen while Watford carefully planned his development and, of course, increased his value. Tonight will centre around this young man and his insatiable desire to score with every kick, no matter where he is on the pitch. If we as team are not on guard, it will be three more points lost. That is my pre-match prediction.

Tuesday night games are great, though. I get down to Swansea with our hardy crew of Kev from Henley and Andy from Gloucester, and the man that is Howard of

Cowbridge via junction 35 of the M4. It's as if we have been once again thrown together in our everlasting quest for success. As individuals our cause would be a lost one, as a team we are invincible.

I stopped for a leak at Sarn Park and was called 'dickface' by a local. What a lovely chap, and worthy of mention only because this sums up our friends from down the road. He made a quick exit though. Not quite the type of chap the more illustrious books on football culture would have you believe exist in East Wales!

Rossi's chip shop was attended, the others floating off with their renewed season tickets and £100 vouchers to spend in the Swansea City superstore. I hope I have room for the extra stuff I buy on the journey home! Superstore indeed! We are very posh these days at Swansea City FC. Basically we haven't gone as money-mad as Cardiff City, offering pearls and jewels for season ticket renewal, but we are offering a bit of March madness. You renew this month and get a £100 voucher of old superstore stock. It's great. People are seen legging it away with clocks, lamps and duvets that they wouldn't have otherwise purchased. I see my mate Jon from Gloucester with a lovely winter coat, and it's expected to be 15°C tomorrow. He'll make good use of that I am sure.

The anticipation outside is tangible. I hear a very local accent shout, 'Get me a fucking Swans lantern, Myra.'

She looked over quizzically 'A fucking what?' she replied.

'A lantern, you stupid mare, you know – a light!'

She calmly turned to the person alongside her and stated, 'What does he want?'

The reply was magnificent, 'I think he wants a fucking torch, love!'

'A torch? Do they sell torches? Setting on fire is what he wants, not a fucking torch.'

I would never have been privy to such a scene had it not been for the March madness season ticket offer.

The game was one of those wonderful occasions when, as you enter the ground, you can smell the burgers, beer and smoke (aye the smoke). It's lit up and is relatively full (for midweek at Swansea that is) and the 100 or so hardy Watford peeps are in the corner of the away stand. A banner bigger than the room they take up rests on the seats as the crowd begins to chant. My good mate Ian Williams joins us in the seated area midway and centre in the East Stand. He explains how we will ease our way through this game and put behind us the dreadful performance that was Scunthorpe. We start like a train and I agree, we look like champions. Slick passing, Dyer wizardry, Sinclair tantalising them and the crowd, all finished off with a Stephen Dobbie scorcher. Get in there! It's on. Unlike the Doncaster victory, we press on and look to increase the pressure. Then it's over.

I look to Alan Tate, a supreme Swans man, for inspiration and then to Neil Taylor and Ashley Williams. I see fear and nerves and feel their trepidation. And Rangel is nowhere. We are losing our composure and confidence again. The slick passing turns into bobbling balls and unsure feet, the atmosphere changes, and the games turns on its head. Gower is lost, as is Joe. I am lost as well, and at half time we breathe a sigh of relief. That man Graham nearly scored twice and, if it wasn't for Dorus, he would have. The second half passed as a blur of yellow as Watford busied themselves around our midfield, pressing on and dictating the next move. The inevitable happened and luckily for us only happened once. And Danny Graham delivered it. 1–1 is the final score and I take some comfort from this. Had this been last season under Paulo we would have lost, that much I do know. I am angry at the end, only because I know we are better than this, much better. On reflection as I write this last piece as I do after a game I am more conciliatory – we gained a point is what I am saying, I am sure if I say it enough I will convince myself that this is true. A look at the league table as I did after the loss at Scunthorpe is pretty inspiring, though. Swansea City are still second, and after two miserable results, we still hold the cards.

If Ashley has the desire to tweet tonight I hope he thinks long and hard about what it is that he wants to say. He needs to know that at times it is about the team, the fans and, of course, him. And what he says can have great impact – on some.

Our unhappy crew of England-based Jacks find solace in each others' company. Hence our perilous journeys and sugar-coated love of the Swans. I bet you're thinking 'how dare he have an opinion about our heroes in white, especially our Ash.' Well, I see him as a solid professional, true to the jersey he wears and the team that pay him well. I like him.

I say England-based Jacks, but what I mean is a decent number of England-based Jacks complimented by a further decent number of Swans fans who have gone home for one reason or another. This calls for a train journey to Derby. Its nine o'clock on a pretty overcast but dry day and I find myself and six others on platform two at Gloucester station. We have our Derby match tickets in our pockets and first-class train tickets as well for the journey. The promise of complimentary bacon butties and coffee does enough for us to fork out an extra £8 for first class travel. Howard of Cowbridge is already on the train, having boarded in Cardiff – he looks lost. Standing by a small eight-seater compartment he nods in its general direction. 'That filthy sty is first-class mate,' he says. I peer inside and see a snotty 'train host' beavering away on his mobile phone, and a disgusting compartment. It's too warm and smelly for even us. I am appalled and a stiff letter will be written come next week. I seize the day and take a seat, emptying my beers on to the table, as do the rest of the team. The train host looks up and before he can say anything I tell him 'Not a word mate, we are adding to the ambience, you keep your head down and do the same.' He finally drags himself to his trolley and informs us nothing is complimentary and there is no hot food, we have been rumbled again, but not before he is relieved of his biscuits and gently reminded that the coffee is complimentary. He agrees this is so, and we munch through dry biscuits only satisfied by London Pride and Tomos Watkin Swansea ale.

I do enjoy our intermittent journeys across the country to away grounds by train. Derby for most of us is a direct journey taking an hour and a half. And on the end of it is a fine ale house called the Brunswick just by the train station. An oasis indeed. This wonderful tavern sells its own ales plus many more – fine prices and finer ales. To compliment all this they have a cracking idea for food upstairs. Serve it simple and tasty. You can't go wrong here my friends. Well you can, and many do, it's called over drinking, and this often happens to us at this type of hostelry. In our younger days, when we assembled in Cheltenham for coach journeys around the lowest of the low (that is league grounds of the lesser divisions), we used to get hopelessly lost – in local beer. Never any malice, just high spirits and a deep regret that a football match breaking out in the foreseeable future will spoil our afternoon's drinking and companionship. It doesn't feel much different today in Derby, a bad sign if ever there was one.

After a brisk and slightly staggery (for some) walk along the river we get to Pride Park and into the very well-attended away end. Much singing takes place, and as ever the over-zealous stewarding at the ground takes a hold, seeing this support for the away team as an affront to reasonable behaviour. This has often been a problem at Derby, and always ends up with the stewards getting more than they bargained for. I still can't work out why they think a fluorescent jacket gives them superhuman powers. My recent trips to places like these tell me to avoid conversation with them and if confronted request quite courteously that they 'go away'. Now I ask this question 'is this customer service?' I watch the odd person being ejected, some for just reasons, and others simply because they are there or get in the way, and then as the local constabulary arrive and signal to all its best to leave be, it stops. The stewards, like little children move back to their perches, and the police take over. Three of those manhandled by the Pride Park pack are dusted down and returned to their seats and order is restored. But not so on the pitch.

Derby have come up with a cunning plan. Howard describes them as a pub team, and I can see why. However, today they are a pub team with a plan – to close down the space that the Swansea back four desire, and hit them hard. For Tatey and Ash this is a problem, they are not the quickest and they lose possession on at least three occasions during the first few minutes. Then Ash drives the ball with precision into the back of his own net, mistaking the goal for Dorus the keeper. 1–0 down: Derby tactics rubber-stamped. Now instead of retiring to the bar as most pub teams do, their plan now descends into what they know – fouling, arguing and spoiling the game. Someone should tell them that this may well be the reason why they are where they are in the league. But this time it gets results, and encourages the ref to join in as well. I wonder if he has 'Derby' tattooed somewhere on his person. Not helpful. Swansea City as a team and as a unit are appalling.

The second half does a little to restore faith, but despite Sinclair's runs and Beattie coming on for a downbeat Dyer, we only get one back. The goal is a wayward cross from Rangel, poached well by the other sub Darren Pratley at the far post. The cheers are muffled, because Derby have already bagged a second at the other end from a corner. So poor is the defending that you wonder if this team really is in second place in the Championship and looking at promotion to the highest league in English football. I can't and won't applaud that type of performance, and by the time the team have unhuddled themselves many of the 2,000 or so travelling Swans have gone. They can clap an empty stand all day as far as I am concerned. They all earn fortunes, and today have let themselves and me as a fan down. And I am £150 worse off for the torment. Three games in a week, one point gained and misery all round. Mine's a double.

Chapter Twelve

Flowers of Romance

Being a converted fool I long for next Saturday as soon as Monday morning has arrived. I yearn for the journey and the companionship. Talk with everyone centres around putting things right and getting into Nottingham Forest on Saturday – in some style. It's mid-March and the end of this game signals a two-week break for some, although nine Swans players will be involved in under-21 and full international matches. It's a sign of a team which is ever-improving. The two-week break features Wales v England at the Millennium Stadium – every copper's nightmare. So on Saturday it's Swansea v Cardiff v Wales v England. And for anyone scratching their head at such a thing, trust me, it's true. As fans we find it very hard to come together as fellow Welshmen and women for an international game, nigh on impossible for some, yet Chelsea, Millwall, West Ham et al all seem to compromise some ground for their country when they meet and support them. In Wales? You've got no chance mate. I'll turn to this later, when the game is closer.

Swansea City don't come out too well on customer service matters in a survey this week and that doesn't surprise me. Not that it's Swansea City, just that football doesn't understand such a thing. They are more interested in your coin and your loyalty. What other business will employ stewards who will punch your face in if you don't sit down? They know that most of you will turn up weekly, and most clubs are short-sighted when it comes to improving that average attendance figure. That's my opinion after forty years of watching Swansea City and football. I do see certain changes at Swansea, but I don't see them encroaching anywhere near those places they should do – all over Wales, including Cardiff. That's what good businesses do, they break down boundaries. I've seen large numbers of Swansea fans getting on trains from Cardiff for home games, so there is a support there which is far more than is appreciated, trust me. And the valleys closest to Cardiff are spilling over with Jacks – the club just cannot rely on this support forever – it has to increase awareness.

Swansea City need to go deeper into Wales, to nurture the support and increase the passion that a child will have for a club no matter where they go or what they do. That support needs to be recognised and discovered, and Huw rightly states these facts in the media this week. He can be perceived as a dour man at times in conversation, carefully thinking through his responses. He is who he is. But I am not feeling a lot of enthusiasm from him – maybe like me, our Huw is tired.

There is a shining light this week though, Brendan has raided Chelsea again and got us that young striker by the name of Fabio Borini, not twenty-one until the end of the month and a real goalscorer in the reserve team at Chelsea. It's a positive step and an alarm bell firmly rung in the head for the likes of Craig Beattie and Luke Moore who haven't impressed in goal returns this season. He looks a busy boy, and if he is to be relied upon over the next nine games, he could well write himself into Swansea folklore without tweeting, shouting or throwing his toys out of his pram in any way.

So here we go again. Today's game against Forest feels very similar to the Leeds game. It's a bright day, not only for the trip down Swansea way but for the lads in the car. Our Kev is off to Fuerteventura next week and is in holiday mode again and Andy Conks is joining us at Aztec just off the M5 for the trip west as well. Andy used to be a regular with us back in the 1990s when he lived in Bristol and I recall a trip over to Hull City in 1994 – that day stays with me. We hired a minibus from Gloucester and got up to Hull early with our Dave scoring a good pub pre-match. Dave Naylor was a diamond in the pub-booking stakes back then. Sourcing pubs from his good ale guide enhanced the matchday experience no end. On this day, and it was late August as I recall, we actually won 2–0 at the old Boothferry Park ground. A good four hundred or so travelling supporters celebrated in style after a very decent victory. Andy celebrated far too well, and ended up doing a one-man pitch invasion, being chased around by stewards. It's funny how the emotions can change you in such circumstances. There are many examples elsewhere. I am sure you have your own personal experiences of overexuberance. The Hull stewards grabbed a hold of Andy and dragged him away and his face changed from celebration to horror as it dawned on him the error of his ways.

They only chucked him out though, it was the end of the game more or less, and he met us outside with the usual Hull City Collective departure crew waiting to do any stragglers a bit of no good. He was absolutely mortified, that is the best way to describe it. He felt he had let everyone down, bless him, there was no consoling him. What he thought would happen is beyond me, even today. We never seemed to have a good relationship with Hull City fans, and that went on for some years.

Moving onwards to today, the sun is again shining Leeds United style, and the Globe public house is the choice of the day for some real ales. I feel very confident that we could turn over a Forest side that had hit a bad patch of form. But they are a decent side, and seem to have signed as many strikers as the rest of the division have in total. And I rate their defender Wes Morgan no end. Today, if Fabio Borini goes at full tilt, as we know he can, Wes will have his hands full. Borini's debut feels like the Tony Bird debut of 1997 when he signed for us from Barry Town. They were then a major Welsh League force. Tony scored twice against Brighton that day and earned a few of us some big bookie payouts opposite the Builders, the then meeting place for the England Jacks. He was something like 16/1 to score as well! Another stunning debut of note was Leon Knight's against MK Dons. He bagged a hat-trick that January night in 2006. For me today has all those ingredients, I have great faith in Brendan's ability to seek out players he has previously worked with. Scott Sinclair has proved to be a diamond – will Fabio Borini do likewise?

I shouldn't have been so concerned, Fabio literally tore Nottingham Forest to pieces. With the stunning wing play of Nathan Dyer, Scott Sinclair's foraging runs (and goal) and a well-marshalled midfield, the Swans destroyed their top-six rivals. It was only when Brendan tinkered slightly with the introduction of van der Gun and Britton that we seemed to lose some direction. I will say this though, we were always up for another goal with the many breakaways we had throughout the game. Borini bagged a brace and Sinclair tormented Forest's defence before despatching a cool finish beyond Northern Ireland keeper Lee Camp. Forest did manage to hit back though, and Paul Anderson scared us to death at the end hitting a post when it was 3–2. I spoke to a Forest fan after the game, who told me had they scored he would have been totally embarrassed (though happy), but they just didn't deserve anything from the game. Forest manager Billy Davis agreed, 'We deserved nothing, and that's what we got.'

The manager of the month title given to Brendan at the start of March has been exorcised at last. The previous three results have been very disappointing. Today, the Swans literally flew. The message from Swansea to Forest, unspoken but clearly sent, was the exclusion of Darren Pratley on the pitch. Darren has been courted by a number of clubs, and many Swans fans have been annoyed by his decision not to sign a new contract. Some were booing him (I will say some, it was only a few) and that for me is counter-productive and uncalled-for. In the main he has done well for the club, but every time his head gets turned, he loses form, that's noticeable to us all. The fact he made no appearance today can have many connotations for him and the club too. For me there is a long line of ex-Swansea City players who have seen the grass as a greener prospect elsewhere. Darren seems to be one of those players. Andy

Robinson was another, exactly where did he end up? – at Leeds United and out of favour and latterly at Tranmere Rovers. A career ended by his own decision to leave the Swans who had been promoted to the Championship, Leeds being in the League One play-offs. He could have gained a few more years with Swansea had he signed his contract. He chose not to, and when Leeds failed in the play-offs he remained a League One player. Swansea refused to offer him another opportunity after Leeds' play-off loss, leaving him with no option but to take up the move to Leeds. He has been quoted since as this being a move, in hindsight, he wished he hadn't made. Robbo had been with us since the days of Flynn, so in a way I can see his desire to ply his trade elsewhere. What he forgot to factor in was the Swansea effect. He had found a home, an adoring support and a way of life that he couldn't transfer to another club. In Wales, as I have said already, we have a mass media concentrating on two clubs representing one whole country. That ain't quite the same anywhere else. Players get caught up in this and think that's the norm – it isn't – and they quickly find this out.

Steve Jones won't mind me mentioning his move back to Cheltenham Town after sterling Swansea service. He couldn't believe the difference in the interest in his home town club – he told me it wasn't comparable at all to being at Swansea. I know other players who will tell you the same. Where else do countless newspapers, TV programmes and radio shows concentrate so heavily on two teams outside of the Premier League? Do footballers get the right advice? I think a broader view was needed with Andy Robinson, and it wasn't available to him. Or maybe he wasn't able to comprehend things as they were. Either way, he lost his Swansea opportunity, burned his bridges and many fans have not forgiven him. Things maybe are slightly different for Darren Pratley – he could secure a Premier League squad place. At the moment it's West Ham in the driving seat, next week someone else I am sure. If it is West Ham, will he be a Premier League player next season in any event? Think hard about this Darren is my only advice.

Borini's performance and the way it was received by an 18,000-plus crowd has brightened up our trip home, and even one of the most disturbing sights of recent trips fazes me not – a small coach packed with Forest shirt-wearing kids all in unison flicking 'V' signs along with a very elderly gent in stereotypical Uncle Fester mode doing the same. Was he in charge of them? I hope not.

The next focus is the Wales v England game at the Millennium Stadium. The hostile press go to town on druids and sheep and the responses will only be felt in the bars and pubs of Cardiff – physical at times I have no doubt. We live in hope of just one Welsh victory. Just one.

Chapter Thirteen

Can We Buy an Away Win, Please?

Of course it was never going to happen. England came to Cardiff's Millennium Stadium with a clear objective of securing a lead and building upon it. Adrian Durham was right again on Talksport, England are far better in all departments, bar maybe Ramsey in a midfield role. The game itself displayed Wales as a national side not even ready to start a rebuilding process – it hadn't got to that level yet. Surprisingly though, for some, they still felt before the game that Wales could beat England. I didn't, and never did think that a positive result for Wales would ever be on the cards. A relatively full stadium cheered on the home side, and even though the media decided to concentrate on the negatives of fans booing national anthems and Capello's inability to manage a team, overall the result – a 2–0 win for England – was right. I met with some chest-beating after the game, and asked an England fan if he genuinely felt a 2–0 win over a side as poor as Wales was anything to be proud of. He hesitated, drank from his can of full-strength lager and shouted 'Ingerland, Ingerland, Ingerland!' Very well summed-up my friend.

For me though, as a Swansea City fan, a big problem was the continued inability of Wales fans from different clubs to mix – Swansea and Cardiff predominantly. The day's events unfolded as groups of Swansea City fans and maybe those considered less desirable from West Wales, as predicted, turned up in large numbers. So much so that the South Wales Police kettled (the phrase of the year) a group of two hundred known Swansea supporters and led them to

a bar in the city centre where they were detained until after
the match. A friend of mine has mentioned that Cardiff
City's known hooligans went about their business as usual,
and many known faces attended the game unheeded and
without restraint. Fair? It seems that the police action
taken did prevent what was a clear plan by a certain
section of Swansea fans to disrupt and confront Cardiff
City supporters, as was clear from YouTube footage put
on the web quickly afterwards. What I am not sure about
is whether this will do anything for future relationships
between the fans. There doesn't seem to be any relationship
at all bar the few I know personally. So any bridge-building
has been damaged by the actions of these fans, and will no
doubt hinder any chance of dropping the 'bubble' aspect
of the local derby games. For genuine fans, and by that I
mean those who support Wales and not their club side at
international events, the national side for both Swansea
and Cardiff supporters can be a dangerous proposition –
a Welsh divide tainted by hooliganism is never far away.
And that does more than taint our national game. Mind
you, holding up your petrified five-year-old son in a Cardiff
shirt and shouting 'You Jack bastards!' to the Swansea fans
isn't the way forward either. The mindset of this sort of
individual I am yet to get to grips with, and many friends of
mine tell me I never will. I can understand the tribal rivalry
of football, and the community aspect of representing your
town or city, but did that child need to be that involved?
I was appalled, and vowed never to enter the Millennium
gates again for any Wales game. Enough is most certainly
enough.

I will make no further comment on the game, except to
say that I am more than thankful that club football returns
this week and already nigh-on 1,000 tickets have been sold
for the away section at Deepdale for Preston North End v
Swansea City. There are a few days left and of course, as
ever, the option to pay on the day should see another very
large Swansea City away support. Enthused by his nation's
under-21 victories Scott Sinclair of England returned to
training, as did Fabio Borini of Italy, both unscathed and

both as goalscorers. Fantastic news for both young men who have so much going for them as young people who have been handed a skill and ability that will earn them millions of pounds over the coming years. Fabio has explained his celebration as well to the uninitiated. He celebrates in the same way as his hero Filippo Inzaghi: hand in mouth and arm outstretched. And if Fabio gets half the plaudits over the coming years as Inzaghi, Swansea City could be onto a real winner. To cap off a positive week, Tamas Priskin has signed for the Swans until the end of the season from Ipswich Town. Their fans don't rate him much in the same way as Luke Moore and Craig Beattie were not rated by West Brom. The manager believes he has secured a signing that will elevate us even further in to the promotion picture. I remain to be convinced.

The trip north to PNE is a long one from Swansea, although not so bad for me, and once again I am in the company of some most illustrious gentlemen. I am very lucky indeed.

Preston North End have a real tradition in the Championship, they have had many years of trials and tribulations as a club. They have flirted on a number of occasions with Premier League football, and my mate Preston Pete will tell you that the play-offs for them have been a catalogue of one misery after another. However, I reckon today they would prefer, I am sure, to be in a play-off spot and going for automatic promotion like Swansea City, than to be at the very foot of the table scrapping for their Championship lives.

This game brings with it a great amount of fear for me, as the previous two away games at Scunthorpe and Derby have been a comedy of errors and total lack of form. Dorus needs to be more demanding and commanding in certain situations – for me he can be too laid back at times, though for all these things, I still rate him very highly as a keeper. He has to be the best we have had since Roger Freestone left the fold in what can only be described as a ridiculous fashion seven years ago. However, we won't go there, because too many people will be running for cover won't they? The defence needs stabilising too. Poor old Alan Tate is looking tired and I can't help but wonder if he should be rested for today's game. It's only at the last minute I learn that Angel Rangel is poorly, and Tate will play at right-back. I think this weakens us because Tatey needs some time off. Garry Monk is back, so there has been much rejoicing in Swansea ranks at the return of our club captain. I'm not so sure though, he has been away for some months, and an immediate introduction into a Premier League-chasing side (a level that requires extreme awareness and fitness) worries me. I think Brendan has got this wrong and instead of filling up on strikers should have been looking elsewhere for defenders too. If Alan Tate struggles and we give the ball away too much in midfield via Mark Gower – a vastly improved player but still with certain inadequacies – we could be in bother again. I fear that Iain Hume will be on his game as well. He is a class act, and the new manager Phil Brown has PNE fired up big time. He has a very good squad of players that needed inspiring, and unfortunately for the Swans, that inspiration has happened since Phil Brown has arrived at Deepdale. Players like Adam Barton, Paul Parry, Keith Treacy, Darren Carter and Nathan Ellington will cause us some real troubles this afternoon, and we really have to be up for this.

Swansea City have suffered this season from what I believe is overconfidence; others have said it is arrogance, and at times I think our constant passing game causes us more trouble than if we were to change tactics now and again. The manager would tell you we do. However, if our opponents pressurise the back four, we do struggle (cases in point being Derby away and Bristol City at home) or if the pitch is just about playable we lose games (like at Scunthorpe). Likewise, if the desire of our opponents is that much greater than ours we lose too (as we did v Portsmouth at home). I haven't mentioned yet that when the opposition is of a better quality we also slip up (QPR away). Some will tell you that the attitude displayed against Leyton Orient in the FA Cup signifies our arrogance, and that we got all that we deserved. I think we clearly displayed a lack of desire that day and expected to win the game, and got stung. Either way, the main question in my mind is, has Brendan learned from recent experiences, has he applied experiential learning to what he has witnessed of late, and changed things as a result? He is the manager, and it is frustrating to see him at a loss for words when the going gets tough. Reading fans know about this. I hope he gathers himself and displays no weakness at all for the coming six weeks.

We need to bring with us the guile and ability displayed against Nottingham Forest and Leeds United, along with the creativity seen at Ashton Gate in a superb performance not that long ago. Fans are saying that wages need to be earned and the players, regardless of tender ages, need to be strong. Sadly that didn't happen, and once again Swansea City as a unit were smashed into the ground by sheer desire. I hate to say I told you so, but I told you so.

Iain Hume destroyed us as he was allowed to waltz through our patchy and uncommitted defence time and time again. The Dorus de Vries early shocker show reappeared and he brought down Billy Jones, another great player in my humble opinion, on just three minutes, and from my position of self-evolving prophecy we never, ever recovered. The assault was relentless, and even Ashley Williams' fourth goal of the season did nothing to convince me this was to be our day. Yes, Gower hit the crossbar – he has hit the woodwork more times than any player I know – but so did PNE on two occasions. Their winning goal from the mercurial Hume was a farce. He walked through quality players like Williams and Monk and scuffed a shot through Dorus's legs. The game was lost, and Dorus has to take some of the blame if that's what we are into here. However, Preston deserved it – regardless of Dorus's antics they deserved all three points hands down. Not one Swans player deserves any mention at all; they were quite simply appalling. I have said before that when the Swans batter teams to death, when it works and goes to plan, we are unbeatable. And I hear managers searching for excuses when they are outplayed by us. They generally state that their side underperformed, which is ridiculous. I won't use that excuse today because Preston won well, with commitment and passion. They outplayed us, and we didn't have the bottle to reply. As a fan spending a fortune on following my team I want more, and so does every fan who follows their side. I don't care if they lose and lose fighting and spitting their last breath on to the churned-up Deepdale turf, I want to see that. From my meagre wage a good £400 a month is spent on watching the team, so I want that commitment, that desire to win and my passion transferred into those players' easy and luxurious lives. That's how I feel today, and nobody, and I mean nobody, will change my opinion. They have let me down and it hurts.

I can't see straight for anger, and no consolation from friends or family can change my mindset. It is best left there for now, hopefully I won't take to the streets of Gloucester looking for retribution! If I do, I hope they understand that I am a quiet chap really, I just want someone to shout at!

It's now three days after that defeat in Preston. Looking at the packed hordes of Jacks – and there were many Swans fans at Deepdale – they deserved more. Some of my prose may well come with a slant that rushes too easily to a conclusion and ultimate blame, but that is what football is about. Passion. My relentless desire for better and better at the Liberty is being fed well by the board and the various squads since we have been there. However, you will know as a fan of this rollercoaster game, that nothing matters when you lose, and indeed when you lose in a certain way. I don't hate the players at Swansea City when they lose, I just resent them for a while. I pick on the odd one like poor old Orlandi and have a right good go. They are an easy target for me, and for you at times, no matter who you support. Any player or official reading this may well disagree with me at times – that's the way of football – but then how would they know, this is *my* football-supporting life? We all have disagreements and differences of football opinion. We all *have* to take things personally at times, criticism when delivered in the affective state we get into after disappointing defeats is harshly worded. But I won't change it. Take it on the chin, oh saints of Swansea. And consult your legal teams carefully. At this point I would add one of those email smiley things if that gives you an understanding today of my personal wellbeing.

I have sanitised my mind to be able to focus coherently on the task ahead. Delia and her East Anglian regimented Canaries appear on Saturday, a team enhanced by the brilliant Henri Lansbury on loan from Arsenal and who have been magnificent of late. Their demolition last Saturday of Scunthorpe, scoring six without reply, would have had ex-Swan Alan Knill wondering why he took the manager's job at Glanford Park I am sure. Norwich City have been magnificent this season, beating the Swans at Carrow Road early on. Their last-ten-minute goalscoring sprees to win games signal a real desire. Their manager Paul Lambert has them rocking along the league, and at this time, due to the Deepdale demolition, we are four points behind Norwich who are in the second-place automatic slot. Since the loss at Preston, Cardiff City have stolen a brief (I hope) sniff of third place while we occupy fourth. Cardiff destroyed Derby County on Saturday, scoring sufficient goals to overtake us on goal difference. Yes, those missed chances in games gone by return to haunt us again. The Sky cameras return to the Liberty and this is definitely the game of the season for Swansea City.

Chapter Fourteen

Delia – You're Breaking my Heart

How do you prepare for a home game at home? The best way I would hazard is to be able to watch that game on Sky or the BBC this season. Since the Swans' surge up the table and constant dabbling with the top six and automatic promotion, Sky and the BBC have televised Swansea a whole load of times. Not enough though for a work colleague to state that Nathan Dyer isn't much of a player, and to spin his nonsense further by suggesting that we only have one player, and that's Frank Sinclair. It's at times like this when I feel compelled to punch the lights out of the offending person, but this does come with a few certainties, like the sack, or even arrest for assault. No, I prefer to deal with these people in a very different way – I get someone else to do it.

Jesting aside – and before you start, I *was* jesting – there is very little you can do with someone from Thornbury (a small South Gloucestershire town) who supports Manchester United. Like many Man United fans they like to claim that a father, mother or close relative lived there, hence their slight northern twang. Personally speaking he should get his arse along to Cheltenham Town, they need support more than most teams, and probably don't care where it comes from.

I am a bit angry and slightly off the wall today. I can't get along to see the West Ham-supporting punk rock band the Cockney Rejects in Gloucester, owing to the fact I have a prearranged appointment overnight, and can't make the Norwich game either. Thankfully, and not for the first time this season, the TV comes to my aid. We have had too many of these of late, against Leeds United and then Nottingham Forest most recently, both turning out to be wins for Swansea. Oh, how much we need a win today. The lads have turned up time and time again this season when it has mattered, and have thrown it away in equal measure. Today, however, there must be no mistakes. If Norwich and their five quid following take the points, Swansea will be seven points behind an automatic slot and most definitely in the play-off hunt, no more than that. After this we have games at home against Hull City, Ipswich and Sheffield United and away trips to Millwall, Burnley and Portsmouth. There is little leeway for a mistake.

On top of this Cardiff got a very jammy 3–1 away win at Doncaster Rovers, securing the game Norwich City-style with two Jason Koumas strikes very late on. A point there for them was what we wanted, and makes this game even more crucial. QPR surprised me more than anyone though, losing 4–1 at Scunthorpe United in a total demolition and Forest really let themselves down with a 3–4 loss at home to Reading, who go above us in the league before kick-off at the Liberty. Nightmare all round. Reading are flying, and their manager has got them boiling. He is definitely a great manager. Surely they, like Forest two months ago, cannot go on winning? It would mean club records and all sorts for them to go up as an automatic choice.

The QPR hearing is fixed for 6 May and if they do get a points deduction for irregular dealings in the transfer market, it could well mean teams will be promoted, in the play-offs and all other permutations east of nowhere will unfold as the last games of the season are played out in early May. Just how we like it? But only when our teams aren't in it I would suggest. I know QPR are putting a brave face on things, and their supporters are too, but they must be incredibly worried about having promotion snatched from them on the last day of the season if the Football League carry out what is expected of them.

Cardiff journalism surfaces today too, linking Joe Allen with Sunderland, then WBA. I shouldn't be so paranoid should I? I get a text that Delia and her Canaries are all heading west with clear intent of ruining our season today – and they are quoted as genuinely believing they will win. I don't blame them, they have 2,000 fans on the road as well, and regardless of the coach price of a fiver, that ain't a bad support. It's not in the Swansea category of a large away support, but decent by any shout. Our tickets are flying out for the away trips to Millwall and Portsmouth and it's expected that 1,500 will make the trip north to Burnley next week before long hauls in every direction thereafter. Expensive times for any football fan. The Millwall game allocation of 2,200 could have sold out four times over and that's a fact.

Watching Swansea City on the TV is not a good idea, in fact watching any team on the TV is not a good idea by any stretch of the imagination. Especially when you support that team, and the whole season hinges on the game. The whole build-up felt like a play-off final. I wondered just what effect this was having on the players, because it was draining me just sitting there sipping Brains SA and munching on a king prawn curry. It is certainly far better to be there, watching the game in the stadium, and maybe making a difference by being there.

The sun-drenched 21°C Liberty Stadium announced over 19,000 fans at the game, all sweating their fears for the coming ninety minutes, the young and the old, the fat and the slim all boiling hot, some consumed, others just burgered out. The cameras swayed this way and that and the polished stadium and its massed thousands expected and got exactly what these games dish up – an absolute thriller. The Swans started with Fabio Borini up front accompanied by Scott Sinclair and Nathan Dyer, and I was pleased to see Stephen Dobbie back in the frame. To me, though, he didn't look like he was moving that gracefully – maybe his bad back wasn't better after all? Across the middle we had Mark Gower and Joe Allen linking in with a back four of Ashley Williams, Garry Monk, Angel Rangel and Neil Taylor. Just the side we would have all picked. Darren Pratley is again conspicuous by his absence, and takes to the bench with Leon Britton, Tamas Priskin, Luke Moore, Alan Tate, Craig Beattie and Yves Makabu-Ma-Kalambay – yes him in the reserve keeper shirt. Norwich haven't got Wes 'the Hoolihan' Hoolahan but start like they have real intent, missing a cracking chance to the hands of a double save by Dorus. He continued that form for the rest of the game as the Swans took Norwich by the scruff of their feathered yellow necks and strangled them. First off Fabio Borini hammered home a thirty-one-yard free kick, which ensured plenty of comment about how he learned all he knew from Drogba at Chelsea, and then Mark Gower, drove home a spectacular effort from thirty-six yards (I do my homework folks) which Nathan had to get out of the way of for fear of being killed. At last Gower had not hit the post or bar and actually converted what had to be his hardest chance for his first goal of the campaign. Oh, now it was bouncing. Curry all over the shop and dry spare ribs being lobbed at the very sympathetic but getting slightly angry missus who tried to remain adult and sensible. But my joy knew no bounds, the shouting and cheering surely confirmed to the neighbours I was worthy of the next ASBO to be handed out in Gloucester. I would have gladly taken one for three points at that moment.

Norwich had no answer to the onslaught as Borini again should have scored and Swansea chances fell by the wayside, but 2–0 at half time was just what was required. The 2,000 yellow-backed Canaries were very quiet indeed.

The second half couldn't be the same, and Norwich are not in second place in the league for nothing. Elliot Ward (an aggressive hooligan throughout the game) along with Grant Holt (an aggressive hooligan throughout the game), combined with Zak Whitbread (an aggressive hooligan throughout the game) and Dani Pacheco (a brilliant talent who plays with aggressive hooligans) to cause us absolute non-stop hassle and trouble. Norwich decided to muscle us out of the game, and at times it worked, Holt missing an absolute sitter before Dorus pulled off another cracking double save. He is the Dutch Jim Montgomery. I don't blame Paul Lambert for his strong-arm tactics, it worked for Preston, but Brendan had the measure of him on this occasion. When it looked like we were about to be overrun, he introduced Tamas Priskin who in true carthorse style held everything up and in slow motion did all he could to frustrate the Norwich back four. Apparently Nathan Dyer was taken off after reaching the equivalent of three marathons in seventy minutes and Alan Tate and Leon Britton shored-up the defence as we coasted to another big-game victory. Then Tamas, on loan from Ipswich Town, bravely won a 50/50 with the Norwich keeper and scored a third. Although as he did so he was kicked by the aforementioned aggressive hooligan Elliot Ward, it made no difference, the Swans had won 3–0. At the end of the game a collective aggressive hooligan onslaught of overpaid yellow-shirted footballers pushed and pulled its way around the pitch with intermittent handshakes. Norwich City players along with a steward-led Paul Lambert berated and swore themselves off the pitch. They hadn't done themselves much justice and were the sorest losers of the season.

A few off-the-pitch antics were not going to spoil the day either, although Swansea fans charging across the netting and trading blows with opposition supporters is not what we want to see, but I am told the stewards were too busy calming down Lambert and Co. to notice.

As the sun settled and the Canaries flew home, having been firmly put in their place, the Swans hit fourth spot on the same points and goal difference as Cardiff City in third, and just one point behind Norwich, not seven as was earlier dreaded. That is one hell of a difference. The only reason why Cardiff are above Swansea is that they have scored more goals this season. In seasons gone by it has been the number of wins that has decided placings when all was level, but this season it's goals scored, then conceded, etc. It baffles me. It matters not though, because on Tuesday the Swans host Hull City and Cardiff are away at Sheffield United. Luckless Norwich go to Watford, and you never know, parity may well be restored come ten o'clock on Tuesday evening.

The crazy gang will convene at junction 12 of the M5 this very Tuesday and head west once gain to our destiny.

I need to take some time out to convey my thoughts to you on the club, the team, the season and the fans. Swansea is a fairly large city and there can be no complaints when crowds rise to 17,000-plus for home games. That is a fair shout as far as I am concerned. The test I think will be this Tuesday, a home game against Hull City. Swansea City fans are many things to many people: aggressive, passionate, hopeful and indeed thankful for what we are receiving these days. They are also very, very, negative, lethargic, ill-informed and at times totally frustrating. Websites will display a whole host of 'supporters' who react to each result like its either the end of the world or the beginning of a new era. They fail to see the bigger picture – now this may not be you reader, so don't take it personally. However, I am sure you know of someone very much like the sort of person I describe. Cardiff fans are not dissimilar. I say this because there is no way that the supporters of that team can be much different to those of Swansea City – both sets of fans are drawn from the same industrial areas and have the same mindset towards their country and communities. They fail and achieve equally across the South Wales divide. Yes both have some notorious alternative types floating around the ether, but on the whole they are so, so similar. I suppose the main difference is that Cardiff fans believe at times the pathetic hype that surrounds their club. This gives them the belief that they are superior (a worrying trait that reveals more about the individuals concerned than any football team can), when deep down a club that attracts an average gate of 21,000 is nothing more than very, very average. And Swansea fit this bill very well too.

However, there are more marked differences. We have already covered the upturn in fortunes at Swansea City since that near-fateful day in 2003, and this is quite apt because the next game is against Hull City. The board at the club has been quite magnificent. Think about it. As a collective none had any real football skills or ability in club ownership when they took Swansea over with the blessing of the fans. They were generally football fans with some business acumen, but no experience whatsoever in football matters. I won't put all of the board in the same boat – I am talking about the healthy characters who love the club like Huw Jenkins, Leigh Dineen, Jon Van Zweden, Huw Cooze and Martin Morgan. With respect to the rest, these are the prime movers as I see it. They are the lynchpins of the club's success, backed up by a group of others less dominant. I salute them all of course, not as seniors or betters, but as people who have committed their lives to the cause, and stood above the crowd. To be in their ninth year of doing so, having presided over a complete football success story at the club, I think is deserving of personal honour. If it were Cardiff City you would hear it day-in, day-out, but the media don't want to know, nor do they care. That makes the story even more successful and worthy of note. What they have done and continue to do is nothing short of a football miracle.

The squad is ever-improving as well, as is the managerial style and blueprint. In Brendan we have a man who is single-minded in what he wants and how he wants it to be done. He has a methodology that thrives on a plan like Arsenal, Ajax and Barcelona. You may smirk, but it's true. If you follow the team or have watched them demolish sides out of sight at times you will know what I mean. However, like the three famed clubs I mention, Swansea also struggle at times to get the result. The game against Hull City will tell us so much more about the desire and commitment of the players and their ability to work that blueprint out under extreme pressure. For me it is more of a case that the type of football we play will always mean that the opposition get chances and opportunities – it's how the team manages that on the pitch that matters now.

Hull City haven't lost away from home since God invented grass. This will be a test.

In a time of extreme financial awareness let's say, trips to midweek games can be a rushed affair costing not inconsiderable sums to the football traveller. For me and my comrades it is a shared journey that makes it more affordable, but even then it still costs an absurd amount for us fans. £25 a ticket, another £40 on petrol, the bloody bridge toll, refreshment and associated matters can mean the cost of attending a home game can cost nigh-on £100. Which makes the Rossi's experience crucial, and tonight the chips were absolutely pants. They don't need to do this to us. It makes no sense to me that a half-cooked chip from one of the county's finest purveyors of the fried potato should be present in any tray of tea time fayre. I had a whole tray of rubbish, as did Andy and Howard. Kev had gone for the Steve's mini-market sausage and bean composition, followed by a Tomos Watkin cask at the Globe. Right arm firmly in his pocket as he drains the pint away with his left is his chosen method of downing said liquor, even in the very well-kept Globe. The three of us were horrified, and Rossi's had better shape up because this is not the first time this season the matchday experience has been tarnished through unsatisfactory chip-making. I was so traumatised that I joined Kev in the Globe followed by Howard, Andy and others. The Tomos was dealt with.

After a few pints all seemed a lot better in the world as we spoke of ex-Swans players now managing in the Premier League (Steve Kean at Blackburn, well currently at Blackburn, for those who don't know) for instance. He played four games for the Swans you know. I thought at this time I must point out the Swansea City goalscoring record in the FAW Premier Cup. I know Julian Alsop scored a record-breaking hat-trick in the BBC-sponsored competition, so made a note to research it. I have to laugh now as I write this post-match – the FAW Premier website is now available in Japanese. Brilliant, and says all that is needed to know about that competition.

The sun is out, but there is a chill in the air and I am trying to work out what the crowd will be like based on the amount of people outside the pubs by the ground. The outlook people-wise is not good. And later this was confirmed as just under 15,000 bothered to turn up, and a loss of fanbase from Saturday of 2,500 bodies was duly noted. You get what I am saying now from my previous comments about the Swansea City support. The city can do much better, and will do I am sure if this season does end up as a complete success. But it's now, tonight, against Hull City where these ne'er do wells and glory-seekers are needed. Throats lubricated, er . . . well, ready to sing anyway, and a full house would possibly be worth the extra goal for this fixture, and tonight I feel as if we will need an extra goal. In fact I am certain.

It is a splendid setting, our Liberty Stadium, a great theatre that even with 15,000 hardy souls inside gives the impression of so many more. The atmosphere is good and a gathering of two hundred or so from Hull and a flag stating 'The Ghetto of excellence' screams some insider joke. The drummer is here, and the game starts in usual fashion. Like Saturday, Swansea are on the back foot. Hull City display immediately why they haven't lost for some fifteen games away and I sense this is going to be a hard slog. I am reluctant to get dismissive about this part of the season. It has to be said that every team has a wobble, but the better teams wobble less than others and overcome the fear of a bad losing streak. Hull City have been fair game for the Swans over recent times, we do seem to excel at home against them and tonight we need to more than ever. These night games though . . . they are not going our way this season.

We all agree in the East Stand that any result will be good, but we could really do with the win. Hull City are workmanlike, quick and direct when coming forward and you can see why it has been so long since they lost a game away from home. They are going to take some breaking down that's for sure. Their manager Nigel Pearson is a great organiser of teams – for me not the best manager out there, but a man capable of consolidating what he has and building (albeit very slowly) on the current status quo. It just happens that wasn't good enough for Leicester City – the team that prefers Paulo Sousa or Sven to a British manager with a bit of steel are clear testimony today that the boss's name is not always the way forward at any club. I can't see Leicester going up, but Hull City, well, if on tonight's showing they had five extra games you wouldn't bet against them. They could have taken the lead, and it isn't until the second half that Mark Gower rifles in a twenty-yarder to steady the nerves. All we need to do now is kill them off. Hull are wobbling, they are tired and there for the taking. If demolishing Norwich is achievable then this should be achievable too.

It wasn't. And as the few celebrate Hull's pitiful equaliser I feel I am ready to explode. As soon as Gower scored we go back into the shell again, passing slowly and ineffectively across a nervy and unsure back four. When it works and it's done with pace it is pure genius, but when it is tinged with uncertainty and a lack of confidence the ball just doesn't seem to be a friend. Ash stumbles on the ball, as does Neil Taylor and any number of other Swans players. The crowd are edgy and it's transferred onto the pitch. Then Robert Koren nearly scores for Hull as does Jay Simpson. Jeez, this is a rollercoaster of a season. The crowd are beside themselves. I try to put it into context: they are a young team, a team that thrives on confidence, on an extreme belief in their ability. They are wonderful this Swansea team, so please, please, please just score one more time for me this season. The crowd get behind them but, try as they might, we fail and a point is more hard-earned than an unlucky gift. We could have lost this game, and cast it aside like we did the home defeats to Portsmouth and Bristol City. Shame. The missing two points to our league total will I am sure feature in our thoughts come 7 May. Afterwards Brendan is defiant, 'four more wins and you won't be asking me too much more,' he calmly tells the reporter. Yes, he is angry, but like the professional manager he is he won't be hanging anyone out to dry, no proper-thinking manager would do that.

The news is circling the day after that Darren Pratley is going to Sunderland and it's at times like this I could despair. Is there a hidden Welsh media agenda here to unsettle the team? Just when they look like they can do this thing we call promotion? This really annoys and grates, and the story is absolute nonsense as well. It is pure lies. Pratley maybe won't be a Swans player after the season ends, we have been there countless times this season, so please, shut up. No mention of any Cardiff City players being moved along though. Probably because you can't sell a loan player. I'm uneasy today folks, I need some recovery juice.

Then I watch Manchester United.

The greasy wheel of football fandom rolls forever onwards, a slimy fellow best stopped with a well-placed bomb. This slippy wheel careers all over the shop, hitting people and hitting home the reality that when the Championship gets rolling, there is absolutely nothing we as fans can do to stop the damned thing. Brendan Rodgers is spot-on when he explains that we threw the Hull City result away. He has obviously had time to dwell upon it. I think it was a point gained at a very difficult time of the season. This is clearly our bad patch, coming as it has with a very effective away losing streak. It isn't lost on Fleet Street, Westgate Street and our man Steve Claridge at the BBC either. The unaware and the uneducated – when it comes to Swansea City – just talk about what they see that day, not what has gone before, and what may well be. Some supporters of the Swans don't like Claridge, perhaps because of his overall dismissive comments throughout the season about our promotion chances. He would argue, I know, but thousands of people can't be wrong Steve.

I am not even going to look at Nigel Pearson's comments from the midweek game as he doesn't fill me with anything other than anger. Never happy, always bloody moaning, now who does that remind you of?

Saturday sees the Swans flying north again to Burnley. The last time we beat them was on Sky a couple of years back on their way to the Premier League. It was convincing too, which surprised me as Burnley has always been one of those places that we found difficult to navigate. I have had a few experiences of the place, some years back when Frank Burrows was manager. It was his last game if my memory serves me correctly and we went there en masse for no apparent reason. The game was another loss, I was furious and gave Frank a bit of mouth about sorting it out. A local lawman also called me a 'bogtrotter'. All in a day's football. The time before that, in 1992, I travelled there with my mate Jon Taylor of Gloucester and witnessed another loss, and Burnley became one of those teams I didn't like us to play that often. That day in 1992, like this day in 2011, was sunny, and that is where the similarity ends. For all the good Frank did with his passing, flowing football and fantastic ability to spot a player, this team today is literally light years ahead of Frank's lads.

This was signalled to me in the first half because we dominated the pants off them. They couldn't touch us, but sadly we still went in at half time at 0–0.

How the hell that happened I will never know. It's getting worrying, all this possession and nothing to show for it. The post was hit as well, but twice this time, once by Sinclair and then by Pratley. Honestly, we should have this wrapped up already. The second half started in a similar way, but with one key difference – Fabio Borini scored to put us 1–0 up. Now that is a lot better, already the Swans are forgiven for an unproductive though dominating first-half display. Then we defended again. What? We have dominated a game for sixty minutes and when we get the lead we go to sleep, defend and completely change tack. What? Why does this have to be? Am I missing a trick here, Brendan? Our man looks touchy on the touchline (I like that). He is walking backwards and forwards. He doesn't look happy. Then bang, bang it's 2–1 to Burnley. Well, that's always going to happen when we concede territory and allow teams back into games. Ash scored a decent own goal and Chris Eagles converted a pretty questionable penalty, but the howling Burnley fans were the twelfth man, convincing referee David Webb (no – not that one) to point to the spot. He needs to have a long look at that decision and why he awarded it. After the game the players came over to say thanks to the travelling support and got short shrift. Gower got involved and disappointed me. After his midweek comments of having to win at Burnley, he is as disappointed as all of us, but Mark mate – no, that's not professional. And over all I am angry again. The players need to realise that when so much hope is given from a team display, and then nothing comes at the end then disappointment will be displayed. Suck it up boys, you're on a lot of money to wear that jersey. And we can't even blame the fact it's a black jersey today, regardless of the club colours on any day – black or white, if we don't kill teams off, then it's all been for nothing. Another £100 up the swanny.

Other results today have sort of helped though. We remain fourth but Reading win at Scunthorpe who have gone from survival specialists to complete and utter losers again. Reading win 2–0 there, and are one point behind us in fifth. This hasn't been a good time for us away from home I know. Scunthorpe, Derby, Preston and now Burnley all surface as winnable games. The mistakes at those fixtures by Ash, Tatey and Dorus are featuring not only in my own mind but in the reflections of Brendan as he talks about being more ruthless and aggressive. If he thinks it, then so can I. Cardiff win, QPR win and Norwich draw. So when I say results go for us, I didn't mean it at all. I am just happy we maintain fourth place with five games to go. It's getting closer with every kick. But we won't make it if this poor away form continues. We will need eighty-three points plus for automatic promotion and at least seventy-five for a place in the play-offs. Today we are on seventy. It doesn't sound a lot, but it feels bigger than that mountain Brendan is climbing in the summer.

The posturing continues with Garry Monk stating that 'we will fight to the end'. Ashley Williams and Scott Sinclair get named in the Championship team of the year, and deservedly so. Garry Monk wants a fight, and Brendan wants aggression. It's all getting tasty, and about time too. All we need now is a Huw Jenkins versus Tan the Man three-rounder and we will all be happy. I am reliably told that the best team in Wales is that team that holds the highest league position at the end of the season. As this is not the case I ignore all other comparisons. Why? Because league places separate the good from the bad. It's that easy. I concern myself in the dilemma of too many snails in my cabbage bed, and too many cabbages in my in box. It's not a nice thing to compare these people who sometimes affect me to a vegetable, but they do need boiling for fifteen minutes and serving on a bed of mashed potato at times. It's just how I feel at the moment. Like Swansea, I need an away win.

Then Leon Britton gets involved, 'Keep the faith,' he proclaims. Jeez mate, I have for more years than I can remember, you don't have to say it. What I want is for you to have some as well. These next five games are crucial.

Then Huw says 'enough'. Nobody at the club can talk to the press. He wants total focus on the game, not on a player's thoughts on anything but the game. I totally agree, the old owners did this once when Phil and I wrote the Roger Freestone book. Because of the lack of respect I had for them I totally went against their wishes and spent time at the Wales international training camp to finish off his book. However, today, with respect gained and everyone on side, this wish of Huw's will not raise much of an eyebrow in Swansea-supporting circles. The press on the other hand, don't see it that way. In lieu of no stories from the club, they gamely endeavour to make up their own. They put some fight back into the Swansea City story of the week and again they print further rubbish about Darren Pratley going to Sunderland. So next season he will play for Bolton, West Ham, Sunderland, Wigan and Leeds. Oh, and Forest. Very versatile is our Darren. This is just more press nonsense trying to derail the Swansea train in favour of the other lot, we know that, they know that and I am reliably told there's a board member or two more than aware of it as well, to the extent that they have made it known to certain Cardiff hacks that this will come back and bite them. More positively Daniel Alfei gets a deserved new deal, a very competent defender who will no doubt feature at the highest level in years to come. He is dead chuffed to sign. No arguing, no debating, no press calls, no complaining, no agents' demands in the press touting clubs in the north-east who want to sign him. Nice one Daniel. And I am sure all you who read this are all feeling me as well. Tidy.

Chapter Fifteen

Shaping Up

Next up are play up Pompey. It's Easter time, bunnies and eggs, beer, barbecues and those 657 chaps with their multitude of Frattons and a park. David Cotterill won't be playing – although on loan from the Swans he can't appear against his registered team. I reckon the other Cotterill known as Steve may well fancy having him along for next season. He has performed reasonably well since leaving the Swans for the south coast. Tickets are flying out for the game as well, many a Jack content that any sort of result will add to the play-off push. I can see the initial meeting between the Cotterills now, 'Hello boss I'm David Cotterill, all season I have been called Steve on the BBC, maybe now they will see the difference.' I digress.

The thousands who make the journey are fully aware that the reception down south, like the FA Cup win in very recent times, will be a hot one. It's a decent day for a journey to the coast. Buckets and spades, lively chat, beers and sarnies are the order of the day. Even the Havants of Waterlooville will be smiling as the Swansea express hurtles into town. It may be referred to as a lingering hope for promotion in the press, but we know differently. They know not of our club and where it has catapulted itself from. How could they? They live in the realms of sheikhs and Russians, big-money buys and WAG-type stories that are as insignificant as they are important to the free press of this country. A poor account in writing of a woman who went at it nine times with Rooney on her fiftieth birthday is a far bigger story than the incredible turnaround led by the Swansea board in West Wales. For us football is the winner; for them – they wouldn't know what a football was unless it had a naked woman draped over it. Swansea City are heading in one direction – onwards and upwards.

I would buy a draw today.

It is evident that the Swans are concerned that recent away defeats, if replicated here, will cause some real concern for the final few games. We don't want to be hanging onto results come that last game of the season to secure the play-offs down west. We are better than Pompey, but they, like Preston, are more direct and more enthused. Mistakes set in with dodgy back-passes. Ash doesn't look right, and Dorus also seems a bit under the weather. Charged-down back-passes and a terrifying inconsistency dragged us through to half time with honours even.

I keep thinking that this is the Swansea way, the way it has always been.

We step it up in the second half and a few chances come our way, though they quickly end up skywards or in the keeper's hands. A clear penalty is turned down – rough justice at this time in the game concerns me more. That point is all we need – I think it will be another point well earned. Other Jacks will say we need all three points, I disagree, this is a staged process over four games now, boys. The strong will survive, the chest-thumping of Leon and Garry needs turning into fact. It has been a hard month on our travels. Portsmouth look lively again and go close through Kanu but I sense a bit of daylight ahead. As Dobbie blasts wide we secured a draw in the south coast sunshine, for me enough, for others maybe not. But with home games to come against Ipswich and Sheffield United these are the catalysts for us – not today's fare.

The game of the day is Cardiff v QPR, it ends in a draw: good news for us all. Other results see Norwich thump Ipswich in the East Anglia derby. It's 5–1 away to the Canaries. I wonder if they were pushing and shouting their way down the tunnel after this fixture? Reading get a draw at Leeds which means we are in fifth spot, five points clear of Forest. It's getting so close now and everybody wants the league to finish. We are impatient and edgy and April is turning into a right blistering month weather-wise too. Will we match it and play like we can with that sun on our backs? Millwall away next. Oh joy of real joy. We will try to stay in our seats, no bungee-jumping for the Jacks. Again another pilgrimage is needed. But before that we have Ipswich Town at home. Jason Scotland is coming back to the Liberty, but will he live up to expectations and remain as quiet as he has been all season, or does he have other wrecking plans in mind?

It's excellent only because it's Bank Holiday Monday and its Easter. The sun is blazing, Borini is amazing and the Scotty dog is wagging his tail. You get the feeling, right deep down in your gut, that this is the game that will send us into the play-offs. We all know that the Swans have it in their own hands, for me it needs a comfortable start and Ipswich Town won't live with us. Luke Moore is joining the party today in a change to the regular format. I won't extend my mind too much on the formation, they are too easily argued. For me it looks like a nine-one formation. Ipswich are totally battered out of sight. Only the first few minutes and a goal from Colin Healy, a well-taken effort, caused a bit of concern. Other than that it could have been nine, never mind a five-goal drubbing for the tractor boys. We could have sent them home with a double-figure defeat to consider. The Swans were totally magnificent as 16,000 celebrated in the Swansea sunshine. Dyer is a player who has run and run all season, he just can't get enough. Borini bagged two, Moore as well got in on the act looking sharper than he has for a long time. Is it Fabio's effort that inspires him this late on in the season? He looked in fine form. At 3–1 at half time, it could have been six and regardless of the fact that it was a slower-paced second half, it was Scott Sinclair who converted, yet again, a very effective penalty. The joy of the victory, the smiles of the day, the tremendous effort that we see here must now march us on towards the play-offs. My daft insecurity of the winter months, the Pompey loss and the six-hour round trip in the snow, the defeats at Derby and Preston, Scunthorpe, Burnley and QPR are distant in the memory.

That evening I tended to my strawberries. They were getting ripe and red far too early in the year. Like my super Swans they looked seasoned and ready; juicy and lovely to taste. Simply magnificent. Thank you lads. You have given me hope that we can do it again. You have given yourselves hope as well, and that above all is just what I wanted.

We are now fourth in the table above Reading and Forest. One point is all we need to be sure of a play-off place. That point I am sure will come at the New Den. After that I am convinced Sheffield United will be put to the sword – but what then? I cannot see any further than that. All I do know is this journey is one of complete madness. Automatic promotion is just out of reach – not impossible but we are on seventy-four points and Norwich on eighty – our potential full total for the season. They need to lose both games to give us a chance. My mate, a Cardiff fan, rings and tells me they are looking dead certs for promotion as well. I can't work this out, how can they be? Because we are. It doesn't make sense.

Talk is turning to QPR and their irregularities in the transfer market. Talk of docked points and chances for us all. Maybe even ten points will be taken away. I laugh – they won't do that – a fine, albeit a hefty one, is all they will receive. I mean, the league can see both Swansea and Cardiff on the Premier League horizon – ye gods – they don't want to make promotion easy for us, do they?

I am all set for a trip to Amsterdam when the Swans fly in to Millwall. The reason is that my band are playing there in the Rebellion Festival, then tragedy strikes as our guitarist's mother is rushed into hospital and we have to pull out. I am gutted – flights lost, no compo and I haven't got time to gather myself for a trip to Millwall. My thoughts are all over the place for our guitarist and the team. I have to listen to it on the radio. A comprehensive service from Radio Wales on the game reassures me that we are not as ignored as we tend to think and the Swans take to the pitch in a hostile but as ever, pretty poorly supported New Den. The commentators wax lyrical (I've always wanted to write that) about our control and composure. They ooze confidence that the Swans are on the ball and won't be giving anything away. 'Hymns and Arias' echoes around the New Den – the Swansea support as loud and proud as ever.

Brendan's statement that the season starts here is sound in my mind: Brendan mate, I don't know where you get them from, are you hanging around with Chris Kamara too much? I am reassured though, as much as I can be. Listening to Swansea on the radio is extreme torture. Being there at the game you can see it unfurl before you. Though not in control of the outcome by being there, you can touch the surface, breath the air – at least have some involvement. Today we could win and put Norwich under extreme pressure come Monday night. I doubt it somehow, but it's possible. I fix my mind on what I know from previous trips and the Swansea support get louder. Come on City, this is our time, let's get it done and dusted. Make next Saturday a party regardless.

As I try to relax, sip a beer and close my eyes, the radio's constant talking projects the players' faces into my mind. The shutters gently close and open on my front room window, the breeze cautiously lifts the curtain, and then they bow in recognition. That man Darren Pratley has scored. I'm off. I'm running through the house and shouting, what must the neighbours think? I don't care. It's 1–0! Calm down, come on City – this is ours. Millwall have no answer to us on top form, they don't even come close. Steve Morison, the New Den's answer to Ian Rush, has his chances and doesn't take them, although one effort hits the side netting. It's these moments that give me hope, more hope than I have had for a long, long time. Stephen Dobbie, my Rangers man, had the last word. He fired a smashing shot into the roof of the Millwall net to finally thrust the final blow into the heart of the Lions. They were gone, their last home game of the season finished. They tried in earnest – firing wide, firing on goal and nearly clawed one back through the illustriously named Tamika Mkandawire, but it was all in vain, and truly I am told, this result was never in doubt. Seventy-seven points we have, and the celebrations from the amazing Swans support can be heard across London. Ensconced high above the pitch and surrounded by more police than the queen when she pops out for the papers, they celebrate. That's my lovely boys.

Swansea City players celebrate Marvin Emnes scoring the winner at Cardiff City. There's a guy in the crowd who just can't resist a picture of Wales' premier club side. *(Photograph courtesy of www.swanseacity.net)*

Nathan Dyer takes the plaudits – he simply ripped Cardiff apart.
(Photograph courtesy of www.swanseacity.net)

Stephen Dobbie celebrates despatching Sheffield United with pure ease.
(Photograph courtesy of www.swanseacity.net)

Want-away Pratley is the centre of attention again as Crystal Palace are destroyed. *(Photograph courtesy of www.swanseacity.net)*

Early contenders for a three-year ban. *Swansea's Got Talent* take to the pitch after the game against Sheffield United. *(Photograph courtesy of www.swanseacity.net)*

Pratley scores from the half-way line and zooms off to sign a new three-year deal at the Liberty. Not. It's 3–1 to Swansea against Nottingham Forest in the play-offs, and we are all off to Wembley.
(Photograph courtesy of www.swanseacity.net)

Young Jacks are Wembley-bound. *(Photograph courtesy of Jackson Pope)*

Old Jacks are on their way to Wembley too! Left to right are: Jamie, Owen, Jon Taylor, yours truly, Dave Naylor, Andy Conkers and Andy Lloyd with a beleaguered-looking John Naylor behind my right hand. *(Photograph courtesy of Daz Pascoe)*

Swansea City fans outside Wembley (in a pub) and why not?
(Photograph courtesy of JackArmy33 via www.planetswans.co.uk)

Fists are raised, the Jacks are in town. *(Photograph courtesy of Daz Pascoe)*

A face in the crowd at Wembley, 30 May 2011. *(Photograph courtesy of Daz Pascoe)*

Scott Sinclair rips Reading apart at Wembley. At half time it was 3–0 to Swansea and game over. *(Photograph courtesy of www.swanseacity.net)*

Nobody celebrates a goal quite like Swansea City: Swansea 4–2 Reading
. . . And now we really ARE Premier League. *(Photograph courtesy of
www.swanseacity.net)*

The joy is hard to describe. The picture says it all. *(Photograph courtesy of www.swanseacity.net)*

The dressing room is soaked in champagne and Alan Curtis (far left) sees his beloved club once again at the very top of the football ladder. *(Photograph courtesy of www.swanseacity.net)*

Swansea City land the biggest prize in world football and take the title
of Wales's premier club side (again). *(Photographs courtesy of
www.swanseacity.net)*

The city celebrates, the country celebrates. And not even the media can ignore this achievement. *(Photograph courtesy of www.swanseacity.net)*

The players who made it happen. *(Photograph courtesy of www.swanseacity.net)*

The fans who made it happen. *(Photograph courtesy of www.swanseacity.net)*

And those who went before . . . Jacks to the core. Love the eyes, Lee. *(Photograph courtesy of www.swanseacity.net)*

Two people the Liberty Stadium will find hard to forget when the excitement dies down and the reality kicks in. *(Photograph courtesy of www.swanseacity.net)*

Ian Williams, Dan and Tom acquaint themselves with lower-league opposition at Legoland, South Glamorgan. *(Photograph courtesy of Ian Williams)*

Tonight I raise a smile and a glass to Brendan Rodgers, Alan Curtis and Colin Pascoe. I could name them all, but you know what I mean. Tonight I smile to myself. We are in the play-offs and after forty-five games of a hard, tough, angry, exciting season. We have made it. We? Yes, I mean we. There is nothing royal about it. The way the results have panned out means we are breathing right down the necks of Cardiff City who have Middlesbrough to come at home. I am told this is a guaranteed three points for the Bluebirds. I am not so sure, is my Marvin Emnes bet a good one? This could all come down to goal difference. Norwich have Portsmouth away on Monday, they will get what they need and Paul Lambert for once is right, it was Swansea City he feared most in the run-in. Nobody else.

Cardiff City as ever, go pop. They capitulate at home to Boro' and lose 3–0. Accusations fly about the players, excuses are made by the fans and as ever Dave Jones gets it right in the neck. The simple thing here is this: going in to the last game of the season, we have better goal difference than they do. If we beat Sheffield United (and you know my thoughts on this) and Cardiff fail to win at Burnley, guess what? Swansea City will finish third, Cardiff fourth. As I have already stated, it's where you are at the end of the season that counts. Not in February, and definitely not in August when half your team belongs to someone else. Although the Swans are in the play-offs, as are Cardiff City, we cannot play each other as either will finish third or fourth gaining home advantage for the second legs of the knockout £90-million end-of-season cup. If we are to meet it will be at Wembley in the final, and I am not sure if Wales can take it. In fact I am not sure football will if that is the way one of us will secure promotion to the Premier League.

Chapter Sixteen

Last Call

I'm on my marks, I get set and go. To end this nightmare there has to be another beginning, like the one we had at the start of all this at the Vetch Field back near the turn of this fast-paced, ever-evolving century. The pathway is now a clear one – it's the end of the season. As the sun rises over my hotel roof overlooking Swansea Bay I am a happy soldier. I have had to try to balance my viewpoint on all that is Swansea City. I speak to a few football buddies who have left messages on my phone. Roger Freestone is one, a person who I have known for some years now. He is definitely a Jack, we know that, but he has little experience of the fandom side of football – he was after all a model pro for many years, how could he be? Talk turns to a Swans v Cardiff play-off final, but I say now this will not happen, and it won't be because we won't make it – I don't think they will. That's the truth of the matter. Their desire to be a Premier League team, and their failure-littered end of season (and last, and the one before) determines in my mind that Cardiff City won't make it, in fact I don't even think they will win today away at Burnley. It's all set up for Swansea City to finish in the top Wales spot in the Championship, and retain our rightful crown. My personal view is the Swans will fly and the Bluebirds will die, quite literally away in the play-off shuffle. Have Cardiff City ever recovered from that play-off night against Stoke City so many moons ago? We will see, their destiny is in the hands of a large number of loan players and the few who I really believe are very decent footballers like Bothroyd, Whittingham and Burke. I'll leave Chopra out of the equation, because in my humble opinion he is no big-game player, and Cardiff have seen this before. If they rely on him in the play-offs it may come back to haunt them.

There is a bright feeling about the bay, the people and the landscape as the city awakes another day closer to Premier League football. The salty smell of a breezy morning washes away maybe three or four additional medicinals from last night's expedition in the bar. I chat briefly with a Yorkshireman who has had as many medicinals as me over the years, and clearly above the national average of fish and chips. 'Aye lad,' he explains, 'there's nought in this side at Bramall Lane for you to worry about, Adams is on borrowed time, and Cork should have repaid his wages years ago, he's rubbish.' I know these two managers from their fruitless and awful times at Swansea City. They haven't improved, and in Cork's case his tantrum towards Swansea City fans before he was elbowed back down the M4 came far too late, he should never have had the job. Tumultuous times back then, led by tumultuous people from a controlling and greedy world. Good riddance.

There is a springlike feel to the weather, my step and my outlook. I am managing to wash away a pretty bad April regards away form, a period of time that with two wins at any from Scunthorpe, Derby, Preston or Burnley would have seen us in the top league already. Radio Wales as ever talks of Cardiff City, but I do like Rob Phillips and Steve James, people who over the years I have corresponded with, as well as talked at length about the Swansea City situation. My good mate Howard talks about the *Western Mail* headline of last season and the Cardiff squad all celebrating getting into the play-offs – 'Let's do it for Wales!' the headlines screamed. Probably the reason why they once again capitulated. I would rather we just do it for Swansea.

My long-suffering missus is with me today, and for now I have to be happy that she doesn't mind indulging me for games of this type. The last time she attended the Liberty was New Year's Day 2007 when we beat Brentford 2–0. From that day to this only Tate, Britton and Pratley survive. The rest are pretty much in obscurity or heading towards it at varying and alarming rates. In fact Britton and Tate are still the ones remaining from that Hull City game of yesteryear when we survived losing our Football League status completely. What must they be thinking today? Leon has left and returned, a foolish move on all levels, confirmed in his returning more than his leaving under Paulo Sousa. Today Sheffield United are already relegated, and we sit proudly in a strong play-off position. I fear for their debutant goalkeeper if we get it right today, much in the same way as I feared for Ipswich last home game. Leon, you proved you can make the right decisions mate, and also that the saying 'Never go back' is just that – a saying. I like that saying though, especially when it comes to Jason Scotland.

The wife's other games were home v Manchester City back in 1982 when Garry Stanley ripped a shot from the depths of hell from forty yards at the Vetch Field as the Swans won 2–0; that fateful Panathinaikos European Cup Winners' Cup home leg in 1989 which ended 3–3 and not forgetting a sneaky call in to Swansea on the way back home to Haverfordwest when we beat Mansfield 1–0 in 2004. One Adrian Forbes scored the winner on eighty-nine minutes. She hasn't had it hard, but as someone who detests all that is football can you do any more than this as a long-suffering husband? I ask you. . . .

A weekend in an upmarket hotel secured her attendance today, just as it did in 2007 at Morgan's Hotel (Martin, not David's). The sneaky call in at the Vetch in 2004 saw only a late night McDonalds at Carmarthen on the way home and Panathinaikos should have been the icing on the cake. Remember? Tommy Hutchinson ran them ragged all night at the age of about eighty-three. That night we was robbed ref! His pockets must still bulge now. At the time I was living in Barry and the pub I frequented then was a wholehearted Swansea drinker. Not even a G&T on the way home after all the excitement of the night did much to colour the picture nor curry favour with her. My wife remains undefeated in Swansea games, bloodied and unbowed you could say, she said to me just last night 'I would rather wash my face in liver than watch football.' Ah, there, just by the traffic lights – I spy a butcher's shop. I assume it will be a raw liver wash, uncooked for maximum effect?

There is no pressure today, and the talk in the pub is of how many goals will we win by. I don't like this uncomfortable attitude that some fans of the game get when their team are flying. It will all end in tears, just like when Martinez left the club. From hero to zero, beware our Brendan you will get the sack one day, in fact it could be that you remain in control of your destiny by changing clubs? I jest of course, but his time to leave, like all others, will come, and when it does it rarely is an amicable split. Ask Kenny Jackett, Brian Flynn and Nicky Cusack. This foolish chat of 6–0 to the home team is followed by my statement of the day: 'I reckon we will get seven.' They owe me. I was in hospital when we beat Bristol City 7–1 in 2006. Andy from Gloucester retorts, 'You have no chance mate, 4–0 tops.' And 4–0 it was. A sterling performance from back to front – Ash to Fabio, Tate to Gower. Goal after goal was a real joy. Stephen Dobbie's free kick stands out from the rest as he bent in a shot from a starting position out wide left. I got this right as he placed the ball, 'He's gonna hit this one.' And hit it he did. Top left out of the goalie's reach, no chance – it was swirling and curving away from him. The Blades keeper's debut was a nightmare. What summed it up for me was his warning for wasting time when Sheffield United were 3–0 down. It was an obscure moment of surrender from an eighteen-year-old keeper in a complete quandary over what to do next. He played well at times, but he will quickly want to forget his debut at the Liberty. 4–0 is a hammering anywhere, no matter who you are, and Sheffield United were hammered. Completely.

The scoreline comes through from Burnley. Cardiff City have got a draw. On goal difference the Swans are third and Cardiff fourth. Premier dreams already. We will play Nottingham Forest home and away in the play-off semi-finals, then either Reading or Cardiff at Wembley if we succeed. Howard is not happy, he doesn't like the thought of a Forest play-off, preferring anyone else but them. I feel confident, though. Stunning signings this season like Neil Taylor and Scott Sinclair, spanning the unknown to the much talked-about are the reasons for my confidence. Under the guidance of a firmly committed and professional manager in Brendan Rodgers the team is in the command of a man who is focussed and talks of groups and solidarity and mindsets. He is clear in his vision and what he can achieve, so magnanimous and focussed in fact he thinks about what he says and how it will be perceived. These are real qualities in a day of managers who are beset with a lack of verbal dexterity, and who rely upon ridiculous footballisms to get through an interview. Just because you have a football background clearly doesn't mean you can verbalise it appropriately in any situation.

Yes, our Brendan is a diamond, easily run out of town at Reading trying to play the football he was known for at Watford. Run out of town by a club who didn't have the foresight, ability or players to play the way he wanted to. At this point it dawns on me that this is Brendan's first full season as a manager. What an achievement, what a pitiful wretch he looked leaving Reading. Ridiculed and laughed at. What price today a Swansea v Reading play-off final? What price indeed for the thoughts of a contented Brendan Rodgers this evening. QPR get the fine that was anticipated but it doesn't really matter, there was no way that they were getting enough points docked to not get a deserved promotion. Swansea are cited as looking at legal advice (the papers straight away get it wrong) and say Swansea are taking legal action. No, the club are taking advice, something the press should do at times.

You can see I am sure that my mind is racing as I write this in my hotel room overlooking Swansea Bay. One thought after another, anger surfaces and excitement rises, emotional? Too right, mush. Tonight we celebrate with dinner and a few bottles of what we fancy. Oh yes, tonight we dance over the glistening bay of Swansea. Cheering and laughing, drinking and celebrating with those who choose at this late hour to shout for the Swans. There will be some that will join the journey I am sure, especially should this end up in the Premier League. Latching onto the success. It happens everywhere. Wales's premier team are third in the Championship, now all we need are tickets for the two legs against the Forest.

Chapter Seventeen

Two Minutes to Midnight

A nd so it is written. Swansea City are to play Nottingham Forest away and then at home. Cardiff City will play Reading away and then at home. The home advantage being the second game, in front of your own fans, knowing what you have to do. I don't rate Cardiff's bottle, it has been a rollercoaster for them and their loaned players. For us the unity felt throughout the squad has emanated to the stands and terraces – only one loan player consistently playing in Fabio Borini, and a brief cameo for Tamas Priskin being the players making any real impact. I suppose the five games off the bench for Jermaine Easter should feature, but only briefly – he didn't cut the mustard, Delia. He ended the season on loan at Crystal Palace. His two Swans starts were not as awe-inspiring as he would have liked, but he did bag a couple. His replacement, Luke Moore, looks a bit more like the real deal. The Swans get 2,000 tickets for the first leg on Thursday 12 May. They go easily and journeys are planned once more by the Swansea Jacks. If the two games this season are anything to go by there will be goals, goals, goals. If these two games are anything to go by at all, then Forest look likely to edge it over the two legs.

The first game Forest won 3–1, the next at the Liberty the Swans won by a Kenny Jackett whisker 3–2. Like Howard I have a few reservations – not as many as a native American, but enough to make me think a bit. The Forest crowd, well I have mentioned them already, are at boiling point for the floodlit game, they are incredible occasions floodlit matches. This will be no different. Forest have spent fortunes through the demands of Billy Davies – he is on his last mercy mission surely? Lose these two games and their board will be as twitchy as twitchy can get.

The roads are jammed, the journey's not complete as the game kicks off and it is clear that many Swansea supporters are stuck in awful traffic so close to the ground they can practically touch it. Many rush in as the game commences, and some far too late to see Neil Taylor sent off after a minute for a high tackle on Lewis McGugan who went down as if a sniper had shot him. I couldn't believe it, here comes the ref, Mike Dean, one decision to make, and he sends him off. That's Neil out of any potential final, but the real worry is, will we be anywhere near it after this farcical start? Dean struts about the pitch, spitting his whistle out and catching it. It is not he who we have come to watch tonight, but you would think that is the case. He's the JLS of refs, the balding man so easily caught in a Swansea/Cardiff crossfire, earning attention, seeking attention, demanding attention. He could have shown some flexibility, but no, not Mike Dean. Then the customary fouls rained in on Swansea players, Chris Cohen committing foul after foul without a warning. I grew to accept our fate. Mike Dean's barmy army was here, in red and white. Of course, these are the thoughts of an irrational man – I am sure Mike Dean is a lovely guy, a family man of great compassion. But at this point I hated him.

The sending-off galvanised Swansea City, it forced us to fight, to think, to be even more courageous. It worked Mike, so cheers. Forest couldn't muster a fart on goal in the first half with one exception, and for me the side with eleven men was us. The eleventh man was terrace-bound, a madding throng of noise and singing. This was Swansea City – we were focussed, controlled and could have been two up at half time through Borini and Dyer. Firing shots in from all angles, Dyer's pace, Borini's positioning and Sinclair's C5 were awesome. Dorus had little to do but palm away a tame effort. It looked good but was going nowhere. Just like Forest. Unfortunately Northern Ireland's Lee Camp was on form and smothered, stopped and disrupted all that we threw at him. I was liking this. The noise in the ground was tremendous, Forest fans once again got themselves confused and began singing 'England' for reasons only known to themselves, the fools. I really don't like them now. This is a club game, keep your songs for your country . . . in fact no, carry on, your country loses a lot – keep on singing Foresters. Tonight could be ours. The second-half rear guard action was one of complete character and would later be referred as the away performance of the season. The Swans were hot, they were organised and a disallowed goal (and rightly so) was the closest Forest got to scoring. Even then, as Dyer broke free, the win could have been ours. Billy Davies later complained that the sending-off worked against them. Well, now I really am lost for words. What he really meant was I am so tactically naïve that I didn't know what to do when that picture before me changed. Brendan did, the reshuffled team, minus Stephen Dobbie slogged it out toe-to-toe. They were magnificent, and worthy of a win, let alone a draw.

The mind games of Chris Cohen, Billy Davies et al meant nothing after the game died down. The Tudgay remarks that we were overconfident and there for the taking were even more laughable. These lost souls had no idea what was coming to them. Atmosphere? They had an education coming about real atmosphere, not what they think is atmosphere in the City Ground. But they think they know best.

Neil Taylor's appeal to the FA of Wales fell on deaf ears, unlike a certain Cardiff City player's similar appeal to play in the FA Cup final. Makes you think even more about our future in the FA of Wales, maybe a better path could be beaten to Lancaster Gate perhaps? Maybe that will be an option (as a full member) come the time when we are in the Premier League, this season, next season, or whenever. Darren Purse having a card rescinded so he could play against Portsmouth in the FA Cup final was made even more bitter when it was revealed that Kieran O'Connor, a Cardiff City season ticket holder, sat on the panel. The FAW really do need to try harder to alleviate accusations of fair play and otherwise.

My mind, like that of many other Jacks, is full of Wembley, second legs, tickets, logistics and complete disorientation. I am no Mike Dean – I cannot strut and spit at the same time – I am Keith, a Swans fan of forty years. I cough, splutter and gag. I recall Wembley in 1997, a pretty poor 20,000 made the Swansea journey to watch a last-minute defeat to Northampton Town. Our only major bash at promotion at Wembley. But I remember the Millennium Stadium as well, and defeat to Barnsley under Kenny Jackett. That day we had 36,000 supporters in the capital's stadium. And the capital didn't like it. But how they danced afterwards. Miles way from the stadium, far away from our misery. That May day in 2006 does not need repeating, especially on penalties.

I just know, I just feel so much confidence in the reborn Swansea swagger I have seen since we stole that point at Portsmouth. I may have mentioned that the Pompey away game wasn't that important – thinking about it now I see that it was. It gave us belief, and this belief is becoming like a runaway train heading straight for Wembley Way. Forest stand in the way, but can they stand the Liberty in full throat?

Just under 20,000 wedge into the ground, testament now that this new stadium needs a few more seats if this travel plan to the Premier League comes off. Steve Claridge is there and my word does he get some abuse – he looks visibly shocked, maybe he should retract his ill-founded comments on this city's football team. He has no a clue about how our passion for Swansea City is built. In these parts our blood vessels still flow with the industries of yesteryear; bloodied eyes and darkened stares greet you like an alien if you make them angry. This city never forgets and gives forgiveness rarely. Tonight is for all that are here, all that cannot be here, and those who have departed – real Swansea folk, not ridiculous bits of skin with no value and little intelligence shouting into a TV screen with no talent and no regard for you, me and anyone else that matters. Just themselves. Tonight think of the likes of Edgar Evans, a real explorer and a Swansea hero. A man who on Scott's

Expedition to the Antarctic died fighting his way home on a frozen slope screaming for his family. He was a million miles from his Gower home. George Grant Francis and Gabriel Powell, oh Ann of Swansea will you hear me tonight? I may scream so loud you will do. These are the legends, these are the leaders, not celebrity and bile but courage and determination. This is an age that few know or care to acknowledge. Real Swansea legends, Robbie James, my favourite and most dearly cherished player from an era of real men and real steel. His memory stays close tonight – so close it burns.

Tonight the industrial fumes, the rising pain and hellfire past that is Swansea and its people will flourish and bring down the statues, smash down the pretentious, and live forever as heroes in this newly shaped history. It is now Jacks, it is time. Without fear and without favour this game is on.

Have you ever seen a ground shake as the Liberty shook when that first goal went flying into the back of the net? It shook on the TV, it shook in the ground like the very foundations were melting. Leon Britton, like never before, struck the sweetest of shots and we are 1–0 up. Then Dobbie for two, it is in melt down, Swansea's melt down. If the Crusaders were to appear on the pitch with shields, flags, swords and war cries it would not surprise me. The magnificent Swans were on fire, the Crusades would be battered backwards by the army of Jack, the Swansea empire-builders. Lee Camp complained and later we would see he was just moaning about nothing, grasping at nettles, straws and pipe dreams. He had nothing to complain about, he was beaten, bloodied and ransacked. He was torn apart as his defence folded in two. The Forest chances were many, but their weakness in front of goal revealed a weakness in mind – they were not up to the task. The first forty-five minutes had surely sealed our day out at Wembley and potential promotion to the Premier League. As predicted the Forest fire came alight in the second half, they came close, hit the woodwork and then scored through Robert Earnshaw, a player I recall who nearly went to Morton at the start of his career when the Bluebirds didn't want him. He looks like Freddie, and most of the time plays like him too. He celebrates, and we know what goes on in his mind, it is the mind of head-slapping and cajoling, but I will give him this much, he never slapped his head to taunt the Jacks. Robbie Earnshaw has Forest firing and we are reeling once again and looking like we could go down to more play-off misery.

Then the hand made the sign. The manager made the substitution and the player entered the fray. It's Darren Pratley and for all his complaining and issues this season, I feel that this man, this strong athlete of Barking, could repay his dues in quick time. He immediately strengthened the midfield, and straight away cemented a potentially collapsing defence. Forest still probed forwards – they had to they had no choice. As Lee Camp joined a late attack, the ball hit the Liberty lighting, losing itself in the glow, only to reappear on the edge of the area. McGugan lined up his shot and swung a foot, he slipped and fell, and in a way this was justice for Taylor, justice for football. Darren Pratley battled heroically to gain possession of the ball running forwards as Camp tried to recover his steps. Hitting the ball from the half-way line Pratley knew almost immediately that the strike was true, straight and most importantly, going in. The ball bounced over the line and it was 3–1 to Swansea. The Forest players collapsed, their best wasn't good enough, they didn't have the fight left to do anything more than play out the remaining minutes. As Billy Davies applauded his team's fans, almost arrogantly, almost invisibly – the Jacks came streaming onto the pitch. It was later said we couldn't manage the 5,000 banning orders. Incredibly, almost magnificently the Swans were at Wembley.

The dancing, the singing the inevitable conclusion to a football season was here, a cup final to decide a Premier League place. Cardiff or Reading – it mattered not, this was celebration time. Long into the night the cheering carried on, no Jack would sleep in New Jack City tonight. Claridge had a bit more – he smiles, waves and still looks confused.

Oh, to be aware of payment for this pleasure, oh to be aware of what it takes to work, then pay and watch your team. The corporates, the takers, the ill-advised and the glory-hunters who know this, they won't care, but their loss is that they do not know the feeling. The complimentary tickets searched out on radio stations by corporate whores who love champagne and wine, not beers and camaraderie. They can never know, they take, we give, our Swansea City cause has always been that way.

I am exhausted.

The next night an awful Cardiff City side once again capitulated to Reading at home. They were quite frankly awful and any chance they had of success this season was certainly lost when the first loan player made their way into their brightly built Lego-type stadium. For me this is where they lost their season, too many mercenaries drawing incredibly high salaries (regardless of who pays). Not bonding, just taking with an agenda not like the one at Swansea of unity, trust and faith. Their players were individuals, selfish, seeking appreciation, lifeless in defeat, lifeless in total. Just individuals with one cause: themselves; one mission: their bank balances. Teams won't win anything that way – it takes more, much more – to achieve what the Swans have achieved. That's how I see it, you may disagree, if you do, I look forward to reading your own book on the whys, wherefores and maybes of a miserable Cardiff season. Indeed I say the same right now regarding my season's journey within these pages. We will all differ in what we see, and how we see it, that's the beauty of the game we all love.

The Wembley tickets flew out of the Liberty. Pathetic predictions of 20,000 Jacks at Wembley quickly doubled, and then some. The Welsh press, media and broadcasters all of a sudden had time for Swansea City. Moronic press from further afield did not know who we were or where we came from – but trust me we were there, in their faces, and now they couldn't ignore us. 'Who is the Swansea money man?' screamed one pathetic headline. Their ignorance as open and visible as could be. We rode the storm, and listened to the news, Swansea City had sold out 42,000 tickets for Wembley. Hear me now – 42,000.

The big club was back. We were Wembley-bound, the circus was coming to town, and Swansea City would face Reading in a sell-out match to determine who had the right to play in the Premier League. Pinch yourself. Pinch yourself now. It's time.

Chapter Eighteen

Wembley, 30 May 2011

After all this, we're going to Wembley. All the queues and the ticket zones, the telephones and the lack of sleep, the day has arrived. 42,000 Swansea City fans will be in a crowd of 86,500 for the biggest, most expensive game in world football – some would say in world sport. And it's the flying Swans who are there against a Reading side very familiar with the Premier League and all that it offers. Many Jacks are just happy that those who don't achieve down the road failed (again) to get to a position that their bragging actually demanded. Personally it would have been an absolute pleasure to wipe the smiles from their faces (again) and purely from a football fan's point of view – I genuinely don't like them at all. It's not that I hate them as individuals, people or as a city, in fact it's a great city and wonderful place to visit. It's the attitude that grates, and that attitude will often not prevail. Football rivalry hits many very hard – as I have said before, sometimes physically, sometimes sadly – I am no different today.

My first issue is how to describe the emotion and feeling encountered on the day we all sloppily awoke after a few too many beers that Bank Holiday Monday morning (6.50 a.m.). Bleary-eyed warriors garbed in white, staggering around in underpants, holding our toothbrushes and with smiles upon our faces. One of our number lets the dog out into the rain at quarter to seven – idiot. The dog is covered in mud, and the house is gleaming. You work it out. It comes in threes and this is number one. Here is number two: I cant find my keys. Why did I leave them outside on the bin? Why did I choose to blame everyone else but myself? I will tell you why . . . I'm on the edge of blissful oblivion and it's catching on. We get away and the self-service scanner in

Tesco is a mechanical idiot, as is the person who interferes to get me the correct change. I look at them intently 'Don't hold me up. I rarely fall out with anyone, but today I am prepared to forego my usual happy exterior and ruin the whole day for us all.' The response is calm, 'Yes sir, I'll get your money from the till.' Quietly I responded 'That's best.' I am on edge and in a quandary. I have not anaesthetised myself the night before as I am driving. It's sensible. I am panicky, very panicky. I may ooze the self-belief and calm exterior of a true professional most days, but today I am a new animal. I am confused, tired, delirious, excited and bloody angry (again). I reckon it won't take much for me to go right over the edge to that pure and blissful oblivion I just mentioned.

I know why this is. It is my body and soul preparing me for the worst. The very worst that can happen. Defeat for my beloved Swansea City at Wembley, and those foolish monsters from down the road dancing in the streets of their losing city on YouTube. Celebrating our loss, as they can only celebrate. They can't celebrate anything else you see – they are losers. Losers don't celebrate, they enjoy the loss of others to compensate. So there is one thing that is driving me today, the other is sheer contempt for the human race, and everything that co-exists around it. I need a Red Bull and a calming cigarette. Then I flash the bloody speed lights on Eastern Avenue leaving Gloucester (this is misfortune number three). Before I even leave Gloucester the omens are all against us, three stressful moments in half an hour, and its not even quarter to eight. We are all mercilessly packed into the car. My brother Jamie is breathing down my neck like a frustrated Labrador, steaming up my windows in the back seat. Andy Conkers from Bristol is continually apologising for everything and proclaiming a new lifestyle that only involves men, while my long-term travel mate Andy Lloyd (curry and beers are his main goals alongside his love of the Swans) is there as is Darren – Swansea convert from our times together in the RAF. A splendid gathering of edgy, partially inebriated, fucking annoying but gently likeable Jacks. We speed away from the grey city leaving a trail of hope and potential tragedy in our wake. Fuck the speed camera, fuck the bin I left the keys on and fuck the dog. Actually, that might be a bit harsh – she's a nice dog.

My use of the swear word is done.

As the sun briefly appears on the M40 I am asked once again by Darren if this is the best way to get to Wembley. We exchange glances, he nods, we speed onwards. We hit London in an hour and a half. Its only twenty past nine. The Green Man pub is our booked car parking space. It has been nominated as a Reading pub, much to the landlord's dismay. He had phoned me the week before to explain we couldn't drink in the pub, but like many Swans fans we were welcome to park as agreed. He was clearly upset at the loss in revenue, what with Reading being a poor relation when it comes to football fandom. And anyway he wanted to party afterwards with winners – not Reading. I look at this an omen, like all of us do before a huge game. I see Swansea banners hanging from a number of high-rise flats as we entered the conurbation, and various Welsh flags hung out by those who don't know why – but they do. Jamie counts four banners as we race onto the A40, and shouts to slow down.

'That means we will score four,' he laughs. I reply 'That means the Berkshire hunts will score five.' Like many Jacks I have become a negative silo in a huge vat of no hope. It rains and rains. Alan Brazil talks about his Swansea mate in Paddington and Ronnie Irani tries to keep up, once again displaying his complete lack of football knowledge outside of the plastic support he shows for Manchester United. He ain't no Salford Red – they are the real Manchester hardcore. The armchair supporters and the home counties majority who follow this Manchester team are nothing to do with my football-supporting life.

As soon as the brainless from Braintree start backpedalling on the radio I take a wrong turn, but we dodge back out quickly and get to the pub in one piece, meaning my mood lifts tremendously. We meet further lost souls from the Cotswolds and beyond. Howard of

Cowbridge arrives with many tickets and the current Mrs Richmond. Also Dave Naylor with his secret coat of many Welsh cakes and daughter, Claire. Ian and Trish are on the M25 having just flown in from Mexico, Carlos the Jackal is prowling Paddington looking for a beer with a bloke called Clive, while Mick Cannon, my good mate from Weston-super-Mare, once again texts me to ask whereabouts is the pub we're meeting at. I doubt I will see him, nor Dai and Chris from Plymouth, but we live in hope. Hubbard of Cheltenham, well, for him there is no chance of any redemption. He texted me at 3.00 a.m. saying 'Where are you Keith?' I can't even bring myself to think of what was in his head at that time to ask that question. Or indeed where he was and what influence he was under. There are many more to meet today: another Darren from Gloucester, Jon Taylor (Gloucester) Kev, Shedload and Monger from Cheltenham and a dark and mysterious chap from Bishop's Cleeve (is he going through the change?) Ryan Hair. Yes folks, that is his name. I see Carmarthen's own celebrity, Dai Teeth, owner of a chromosome too many to worry anyone but the pavement after a bottle of vodders. He is piss-stained through, he smells of a Vetch Field terrace, I half expect dandelions to be growing from his innards. 'Fuck off Cardiff!' he shouts. It is catching.

The Torch pub does a brisk business and then starts refusing entry to Swansea supporters as they are expecting four coaches of Reading fans. None of them turn up and they lose a fortune, good business? No. The morning travels by quickly, the sun shines bright and temperatures reach a respectable 21°C. Ian disagrees, he was on a sun-drenched beach twenty-four hours ago, and now all he can smell is rainy, shitty, hot London pavements and bacon rolls. Jamie has about three of them and I can't keep up – this is no competition between brothers. For me he can win that one before he returns to Belfast to once again ridicule and cajole the tormented souls on Planet Swans. He flies in to Bristol and out from Stansted, not even noticing the five Jacks on the same plane. He is not a complex character, but his mysterious complexity is baffling.

The atmosphere picks up and I really want to experience Wembley Way, a packed throng of fans, celebrating the day, all fearing the worst yet hoping for the best. Wembley Way is covered in a sea of black and white. Do Reading have a noticeable support today? I see the odd scuffle on the steps of Wembley Park tube, police and flashing lights adding to the colour, fluorescent jackets darting here and there as racist chants flow between two sets of non-confrontational fans. Let's be honest most know not of what they do, or why they do it. They just do. Call girls hand out massage opportunities in the throng of beer and flags. What they hope to achieve is anyone's guess. I must admit an hour and half before any football game the last thing on my mind is a massage off a busty Eastern European lady with her roots showing through.

'You like massage Welsh boy?' is the question. Jamie laughs, I laugh, she disappears into a sea of shouts of 'Jack Army' and singing. Dave appears – he is with Jon Taylor. The last time we had a photo at Wembley was 1994 after an Autoglass victory over Huddersfield. Those same faces once again are photographed, each of us aware that seventeen years is a long time in any football supporting life let alone when it's merely a third of it. Dave makes me smile, we often speak. He once attended a game on a dim and distant terrace a thousand years ago with a few hundred others, and as the rain came down he turned his backpack into a coat. That was funny enough. He then calmly reached into his pocket and produced a home-made Welsh cake. Munching slowly through his prize, those of us around him could only smile at the chap who facepainted himself for the previous play-off final in 1997 v Northampton. On the bus from Cirencester he proudly showed us all his clever artwork. He had done it in the mirror that very morning, taking great care to get it exactly right, and he did a fine job. SCFC across his forehead, it was very good and he looked chuffed. None of us told him that his SCFC actually read CFCS. He had done it in the mirror, you see. I'm sorry Dave, but it has to be chronicled here – it's only fair mate.

I looked back down Wembley Way – the small smattering of blue covered in a massive swaying throng of Swansea black and white was immense. This was some invasion. The songs flowed from 'Hymns and Arias' through to 'Swansea oh Swansea'. And not a bad act in sight. Jon mentioned the possibility of this being a Swansea/Cardiff affair. Both of us knew that this would have been a scene of carnage had that been the case. It would not have been an all-inclusive occasion, in fact many thousands would have chosen to miss the game, on both sides, purely because the idiots would have dominated the day. I am so happy I can't hear that awful accent today.

At the top of Wembley Way, I again looked back again at the massed thousands, it was a choker.

My personal view is that Wembley is poorly signposted, and this was rubber-stamped with not one sign for Club Wembley. Now forgive me, these were not my seats but the seats of Carlos and Clive, we left them staring around the many, many Swansea folk, looking for a club called Wembley. They then lost Carl's nephew, and found him again as the crowds battered into each other. Then we are in, through entrance G, into block 103, and into an awesome stadium that would see our magnificent Swans take on Reading for the right to play in the Premier League. It was a show-stopping sight. I hope the players don't freeze. I looked out over the stadium – to our right is the assembled Reading support and all around us the Swansea following: 42,000 of them swaying, singing and euphoric already. I looked at Howard, 'It's not in doubt,' I said.

'It's ours to lose,' he replied. I repeated my mantra as did he. I preferred mine; it was more permanent, more possible, and definitely more comforting. Time passed quickly, the teams came out, and no national anthem was played. My view is we don't have one before each Championship game, so why would we now? I had already heard racist debate on the matter with references to 'The Welsh' and 'Who do they think they are?' on the radio. I don't think Huw Jenkins covered himself in glory either. He stated that it was better not to have anthems, but the media read into it that we didn't want the British national anthem at the game. In realty I would have felt more comfortable with a 'We will go with what the Football League want' response from Huw. Either way it would never have been played after Cardiff City ruined it in the FA Cup final v Portsmouth. More thought should have been put into the whole thing all round. I truly believe it wouldn't have been that poorly received by Swansea fans and many thousands would have enjoyed singing it as well.

Have you ever seen your team play as a capacity crowd watches at Wembley? If you have then you will know exactly what I mean when I say it's a hard thing to compose, to emotionally describe or illustrate in words. I reckon if Shakespeare was a Jack (and who is to say he wasn't anyway?) he would have found it hard to find the exact words to use and the correct prose to describe the event. A moving mass of noise travelled all around the ground, then we had OUR anthem and it boomed around the ground. I received a text from a mate who is a Reading supporter and who was in the blue end of Wembley. It said 'That was fantastic mate, I've never heard anything like it in my life before – what a noise?' The game started and to many a neutral it must have looked magnificent, though for me and my peers it was torture. How can I evaluate anything in this state?

Back and forth, clever and controlled as we got into the game with Tatey dominating and probing forwards and Joe Allen linking with Fabio Borini and Sinclair, I felt magnificent in the sunshine. Glowing, smiling, enjoying the set before me. It all looked okay to me, and even better when Nathan Dyer danced into the penalty area before being brought down harshly. Zurab Khizanishvili is the offender and having just been booked for a nigh-on red card, I thought he must be on his way. Referee Phil Dowd said no, but he gave us the penalty and Scotty Sinclair hammered it home. Oh joy, oh magnificent joy! My brother fell into the seats below, Howard went mental, Andy Conkers cried and the place went off the scale. The cheering exploded even louder than it did against Hull City eight years ago – what was everyone on? It was a bouncing throng of noise that must have registered on the Richter scale.

Foul after foul is committed on the Swansea players, spoiling the game. Then the bullying tactics of Reading backfire when Dobbie breaks free, squares for Sinclair and all of a sudden, in a matter of minutes, we are 2–0 up. I stand still as the madness all around crushes me. I was in total shock. Surely this was to be our day? The white onslaught continued throughout the half and Reading just couldn't keep us at bay – yes, you guessed it we scored a third. Stephen Dobbie, who has had a magnificent end to the season, struck a fine shot from the edge of the area to surely kill off Reading and any hope they ever held of going back to the Premier League. 3–0 at half time. I was stunned. I can't find words now, and never will. Just put yourself in my shoes (Converse trainers) and think how you would be?

I went to the toilet in shock, I pissed on my trainers in shock, I saw a man in underpants with a Metallica tattoo on his leg in shock, and I saw Dai Teeth in his natural habitat. In a toilet, smelling like a toilet. He too was in shock. 'Fucking mentals, Keith boy! I'm off it and it's mentals.' Now I want to see Dai Teeth on Sky as a match analyser, and why? Do I need to explain why? He should be on the TV anyway. There was an edgy silence, many Jacks just staring at each other in total shock. 'We can't mess this up bud,' is one comment. 'If we do, I don't think I can bring myself to watch the Swans again,' is another. But I knew what was coming, like most others who have run this journey before. I know what the next forty-five minutes would bring, and I knew it was going to get messy. A throng of Dutch singing and dancing on the concourse already celebrating a victory made me edgier than I had been all day. This, my friends, is the biggest nightmare journey I have ever been on, I want it to end, to conclude right now. I feel dizzy, sick and exhilarated all at once. What Carl said to me before made me smile. I can't mention it here in full, but it involved the use of man-kinship if that was what it would take to get promoted. Walking back out and to my seat the sun shone so bright, the fans sang so loud and the flags waved so passionately, it surely couldn't go wrong?

Those who know the events that unfolded that second half, those who experienced the total mayhem and immediate sense of loss will sympathise with me now. Within fifteen minutes of the restart we were all at sea. We had transformed ourselves from Premier League world-beaters to a posse of estranged partners trying to get through the last days of a marriage of convenience. I was told a Reading player had been sent off. I couldn't work that out in my man mind at all, how could that be? They have eleven on the pitch, what is going on? I later learned that Jay Tabb got his marching orders from the subs' bench at half time. What a fool – and to think he was right up there as a class midfielder five years ago. In that crazy seventeen minutes after the restart we had been pegged ('scuse the pun, Cardiff) back to 3–2 by a Joe Allen header (wrong goal mate) and an excellently well-taken header by Matthew Mills. Where was Dorus? He seemed to be nowhere. Then Reading hit the post and a stunning block by Monk stopped a sure equaliser. It was absolute, total unadulterated bedlam. Chaos on a scale not seen at Wembley since Paul Dickov and Co. dragged Man City back from the dead in a League One (Second Division) play-off in 1999. That day like this the fans must have felt the same. I remember that game as Man City fans left the ground in droves, including a colleague of mine, only to hear two quick goals go in as they faithlessly walked down Wembley Way. Man City took the game into extra time and eventually despatched Gillingham on penalties. Would this be me? Could I go now and avoid what was coming? Surely it would be better to leave now?

'Howard? Shall we go?' He almost said, 'yes.' I was in a world of total disbelief. We were at the mercy of Reading, we were theirs to do with as they pleased.

Then there's complete silence as the crowd got their breath back for the final half-hour. The calm seemingly restored, Dobbie missed a sitter after turning Reading inside out and the beleaguered and knackered Scotsman was replaced by Darren Pratley – he who from the half-way line can do things we only dream about and read about in books. The midfield looked stronger, Reading looked weak and tired as we pushed forwards – onwards Swansea – searching for the end of this game. 'It's not in doubt,' I said to Howard. He said nothing, he looked like he had been busily rubbed down in an Egyptian massage parlour and readied for the vaselining of his life. Where was that Eastern European lady now, when she really could have leant a hand?

Tate pushes forwards and the whole Reading defence opens up, we shout, we scream as Borini leads across the line into space to receive the pass. The crowd levels rise considerably as Griffin brings him down in slow motion in the box. I see Phil Dowd, he is close, so close to the action, so well placed he must, he must, he must . . . he must give it, put me out of my contagious fucking misery Phil, pleeeeeeeeease! Oh yes, he did, oh yes, he has – delirium, massed ranks pile over and onto each other. It's a penalty, it's a penalty, it's a penalty. It's too much, my chest hurts, my ears pop, the moon is in my face, the stars are hitting me, I'm dying here, I'm falling apart in London. I don't want to die here, please. Not in London, my family won't like it, and I definitely won't. I look up and Scott Sinclair, on a hat-trick, on the day of his life, on the day of our lives, has the ball in his hand. He is calm, I am not, he is cool, I am hot, he is Scott Sinclair – I am not.

GOAL.

Imagine white noise smashing into your head like a train. Please pause from this sentence. Close your eyes and remember what it feels like to be shocked by a passing train, the thud, hit and smash of a passing train as you travel in the opposite direction. Think that for half a minute. Close your eyes.

Because that moment, that brief nuclear moment when my face left its gripper, when my ears launched inwards, my eyes suffered a smashing hot glow of pain: I was gone.

Tears streamed down my face, I hugged whoever, and
danced with whoever. Take me now whoever it is that
decides my life and fate, do it now because I couldn't care
at all. Forgive me for what I do now, because I will never
reach these heights again. Never reach the sky again, never
hit these highs again. Lemmy has gone off in my head.

And we are Premier League.

I hope I did that moment justice. I hope I caught that
moment just right for you. I am forty-seven years of age.
I have endured the footballing life of a bastard from hell.
I have witnessed many things as a Swansea City supporter,
and many things have witnessed me, good or bad, right or
wrong. But this doesn't come close. I am exhausted as the
rain comes down on Wembley's turf. My brother grabs me,
'He's crying!' he shouts. 'Dave Jones is crying, we are going
to get soaked!' I grab him and look at him, my little brother,
little tosser, little bastard that he is and we dance like mad,
drunken fools. The five-star bendy four-step of dances. The
songs, the noise is total. Just total. Dave Jones may well
have been crying, the skies opened up and the tears flowed
from above. For him it was too late, for us it is just the start.
     The rest is described in one word – celebration. I will add
another word – blur.

Swansea City today, like they were at that moment, are
in the Premier League. My life has been overstocked on
Swansea City moments, many have taken me to the brink of
complete insanity. I have been at games where celebration
has been so joyous it has touched my very soul and I have
seen pain and suffering too. You may laugh. I remember
the deaths over the years of so many Swansea faithful, be it
at Ninian Park in an FA Cup replay against Crystal Palace,
or among mass celebration at an end-of-season game in
Rotherham. This season has seen finality touch us yet again,
its madness, its sadness but in among all that shines a pure
white hope. I have grown up with boot boys and skinheads,
punks and new romantics, Hersham boys and Glory

Boys, a Ska-snatched life on a cloud of football madness. Hardcore punks with spiky hair and studded leathers, the Manchester thing and the rebirth of common sense. Our football culture knows no bounds when your team is at the forefront of your mind. The soundtrack to my early life was heartache and hardship, it changed because I wanted to change it. I found solace on that Swansea North Bank. Friends, some long gone, have shared my joy and together we have shared the bad times too. As a young skinhead I recall a chap called Buller, a well-known Swansea lad. He put his arms around me on a Swansea terrace in 1977. He said 'Together we are strong son, we are proud, like lions we are the leaders.' My black Harrington was piss-wet through with rain as we tore across that terrace. One love, one life, one goal.

Swansea City changed me for life. It has done so since I can remember and will do for as long as I live. Today the sun is shining, and the party is still in my head. That will stop, and at some point, hopefully soon, I will refocus and understand what I have been through since that Bank Holiday Monday in London in May 2011. The Swans may go down, they may fly higher than we ever imagined – I don't really care. That's the future, for now I have what I have because it was meant to be. I raise a glass to my friends, my fellow Jacks and indeed those friends that I have from the other side of Wales, Roddy and Co. from the blue half. Your time may well come, stay sharp, but we got here first, it was written and meant to be. I hate nobody passionately, and refuse to divide through difference and colour. Today my friends I couldn't hurt a soul. Because today – we are Premier League.

Swansea 'til I die.

Epilogue

It's quiet now and all I can hear is the laughter of a season in the sun. I have given my heart and soul for the cause like so many have before me. The players that I may have seemed harsh on as this season has progressed must forgive me for my undying love for my team. I am sorry, dear player, it isn't you that I worship, but my club. The shirt you wear is a trophy for you to be proud of, the person that dons the battle dress is a valuable commodity, but they are not worthy at any football club of worship. You may not understand this, but it is so. This has always been my philosophy, flawed or otherwise. I never get upset when a player or manager leaves – why should I? I still have Swansea City and I still have my club. Why would I want a player to stay when he is past it, broken or wandering away mentally from the city's team? I hear and see so many upset supporters when these so-called icons leave. Their egos generating love then hate, passion then grief. Why should this be? I blame the supporter more than the player, the ego of any man can be exploded when a thousand voices call his name.

However, this time around I have to thank the warriors in white, those driven few, those hardy passionate folk of Swansea and its club. And I thank the players too. The most incredible football story in modern times has reached a chapter end. It may well be we have further glory to be bestowed upon us, you, me and anyone else who jumps on the glory train. Who knows? This modern fairytale, this sinking ship that steadied and righted itself when it was battered, used and abused, is now a gleaming vessel and a warship once again. The board at Swansea have been remarkable. If they were in London and this was the same tale it would be blasted from every broadsheet in the land. But that is not the case. The remarkable story and journey undertaken initially by a handful of fans willing to forsake everything for Swansea City is a tremendous tale in itself. For the city's fans to step forward from the terraces and run a professional football club with no previous experience is truly magnificent. To then pull that club through the leagues, not Two, not One, not the Championship, but to the very top on a frugal budget with the fans owning a fifth of the club is beyond words. It is duly noted that those who chose the path to right the exploitation of a club by so many acceptable and criminal faces are the real heroes. The board, those hardy men of Swansea and beyond who collectively saved a club, brought pride back to the city and brought the golden fleece back to West Wales are the heroes. Shed no tears to the brave young men who play, they are rightly rewarded each salary day, but for years this board took no reward, and chose no financial short-cut to their own ends. Their only goal was safety and survival for this fledgling club and this is on the borders of most people's football perceptions.

Whatever they take now will be fine, we know they take because it is deserved not because they pillage and rape, but because when you achieve what they have achieved, and when you have gained for a city what they have gained, then rewards are due. They stood up when the city didn't want to know – when only a few thousand bothered and cared, when no lord mayor nor business dignitary nor Guildhall reception would have even entertained this football club. They were there. And I was too, to navigate the journey as a fan. Having put all I could into the chasing away of the disgusting few, I chose to rest and enjoy the one thing that has remained pure since 2002 – Swansea City Football Club. I am proud of what I actively did between 1997 and 2002, but boys, I am so proud of you, and what you have done, twenty times more than anything anyone else has done. Even if our future was League Two only, that would have been enough, but as I have said before, that is not the way. Not in Swansea.

It is the greatest journey ever taken by any football board at any time, at any club you wish to name. It will go down in history as the greatest journey ever undertaken. I do not jest, this is a real success story, and I thank each and every one of you for making it the greatest, most memorable journey I have ever been on.